The TQE Principal

Total Quality Education for the World's Best Schools

The Comprehensive Planning and Implementation Guide for School Administrators

Series Editor: **Larry E. Frase**

1. **The Quality Education Challenge**
   Carolyn J. Downey, Larry E. Frase, Jeffrey J. Peters

2. **Total Quality Education**
   Transforming Schools Into Learning Places
   Fenwick W. English, John C. Hill

3. **Creating Learning Places for Teachers, Too**
   Larry E. Frase, Sharon C. Conley

4. **The TQE Principal**
   A Transformed Leader
   Richard Sagor, Bruce G. Barnett

5. **Building Coalitions**
   How to Link TQE Schools With Government, Business, and Community
   Betty E. Steffy, Jane Clark Lindle

6. **Teacher Unions and TQE**
   Building Quality Labor Relations
   William A. Streshly, Todd A. DeMitchell

7. **Multiculturalism and TQE**
   Addressing Cultural Diversity in Schools
   Paula A. Cordeiro, Timothy G. Reagan, Linda P. Martinez

8. **Making Governance Work**
   TQE for School Boards
   William K. Poston Jr.

9. **TQE, Technology, and Teaching**
   Eugene R. Hertzke, Warren E. Olson

10. **Tools for Achieving TQE**
    Raymond F. Latta, Carolyn J. Downey

11. **Structuring Schools for Success**
    A View From the Inside
    Mary Scheetz, Tracy Benson

12. **Planning and Troubleshooting Guide**

The authors dedicate this series to the memory of
W. Edwards Deming, 1900-1993

The TQE Principal

A Transformed Leader

Richard Sagor
Bruce G. Barnett

CORWIN PRESS, INC.
A Sage Publications Company
Thousand Oaks, California

Copyright © 1994 by Corwin Press, Inc.

All rights reserved. No part of this book may be reproduced or utilized in any form or by any means, electronic or mechanical, including photocopying, recording, or by any information storage and retrieval system, without permission in writing from the publisher.

For information address:

Corwin Press, Inc.
A Sage Publications Company
2455 Teller Road
Thousand Oaks, California 91320

SAGE Publications Ltd.
6 Bonhill Street
London EC2A 4PU
United Kingdom

SAGE Publications India Pvt. Ltd.
M-32 Market
Greater Kailash I
New Delhi 110 048 India

Printed in the United States of America

Library of Congress Cataloging-in-Publication Data

Sagor, Richard.
 The TQE principal: a transformed leader / Richard Sagor, Bruce G. Barnett.
  p. cm.—(Total quality education for the world's best schools; v. 4)
 Includes bibliographical references.
 ISBN 0-8039-6123-5 (pbk: alk. paper)
 1. Educational leadership—United States. 2. School management and organization—United States. 3. Total quality management—United States. I . Barnett, Bruce G. II. Title. III. Title: Total quality education principal. IV. Series.
LB2805.S263 1994
371.2'00973—dc20   93-40956

94 95 96 97 98 10 9 8 7 6 5 4 3 2 1

Corwin Press Production Editor: Rebecca Holland

Contents

Foreword	vii
Larry E. Frase	
Preface	ix
About the Authors	xv
1. Understanding How the Work of Groups Fits Into the School's Vision	**1**
The Strategic Planning Process	2
Creating a Shared Vision	10
Key Terms and Concepts	18
References	19
2. Involving Both "Customers" and "Suppliers" for Improved Outcomes	**20**
What We Know About Change in School Settings	21
What Makes for a Functional School Work Group?	22
Who Is the Customer?	23
Organizing the Suppliers	29
Encouraging Suppliers to Focus on Quality	34
Key Terms and Concepts	47
References	49

3. Optimizing the Talents of All Staff Members	**50**
How Adults Learn	51
Dealing With School Culture	56
Recognizing the Talents of Teacher Leaders	58
Key Terms and Concepts	67
References	68
4. Being Coaches and Counselors— Not Judges	**70**
Providing Support to Teachers	71
Coaching for Professional Development	76
Key Terms and Concepts	93
References	95
5. Making Quality Decisions Based on Data	**97**
The Concept of Reducing Variation	97
Collaborative Action Research	106
Managing Time as a Resource	114
Key Terms and Concepts	120
References	121
6. Building a Professional Learning Community	**122**
Management by Walking Around	124
Governance	127
Not Expecting Perfection	129
Cognitive Dissonance Theory	130
Having a Clear Vision of the Quality School	135
How to Create a Learning Community	138
Key Terms and Concepts	140
References	141
7. A TQE Model of Instructional Leadership	**143**
Planning and Troubleshooting Guide	148

Foreword

Few people would dispute the importance of school administrators becoming instructional leaders. It has been discussed at great length in the educational literature. But instructional leadership is not easy; it takes great technical and people skills. Too often principals have been thrust into this role without adequate training and without adequate explanations as to why their role should change from manager to instructional leader. Now, another change, total quality management (TQM), is entering education. Because of its potential transformational power, we have modified it to Total Quality Education (TQE) when we talk about schools, and this book—indeed the entire series—is devoted to applying TQE to school practice.

Richard Sagor and Bruce Barnett have distilled the key skills and techniques principals need to transform their daily activities from building managers to instructional leaders. Using their collective experience as school teachers, administrators (principal and assistant superintendent), active directors of principal training programs, and consultants to school districts, they have provided an easily read and practical how-to book principals can use to accomplish the transformation to TQE-based instructional leaders. *The Transformed Principal* provides charts, checklists, and practical explanations of what transformed principals do and how they do it.

Every school administrator knows that technical, interpersonal, and political skills are absolutely crucial to success. However, the *whats* and *hows* regarding these skills have eluded clear definition through decades of theoretical writings. In this book, Sagor and Barnett provide needed definitions and translate sound theory into practice.

School administrators and educators aspiring to educational administration can use the vibrant content, the many checklists, time logs, definitions of key terms and concepts, and strategies for practicing *management by walking around* (MBWA) to break barriers between teachers and administrators and to begin their transformation to TQE-based instructional leaders. When you read this book you will recognize the authors' expertise and their passion for assisting school leaders in achieving Total Quality Education. This book will also open many other areas for inquiry. The reader is encouraged to delve into the other 10 books in the *Total Quality Education for World-Class Schools* Series for other crucial skills needed for the TQE transformation.

Larry E. Frase
San Diego State University

Preface

When Larry Frase first approached us about writing this book we were instantly excited about the prospect. Our enthusiasm resulted from our belief that never before in educational history has the need for quality-oriented instructional leadership been greater.

Most observers and critics both inside and outside the education system seem to agree that the performance of America's schools is nowhere near the level it ought to be. Although this critical appraisal is often a source of defensiveness, it need not be. The educational system is only one of numerous modern institutions that have not kept up with consumer demands. The corporate sector, both the producers of products and providers of services, as well as their counterparts in government and the public sector have in recent years been called to face the fact that their customers are the only meaningful assessors of quality. Furthermore, and with considerable pain, they have come to realize that consumers express their satisfaction or dissatisfaction with their feet and their votes.

Because of this it should be no surprise that educators have followed the path taken by progressive private sector leaders in closely examining the movement called Total Quality Management. At its heart TQM is not a particularly complex idea. Generally, it involves a deep systemic commitment to the now famous 14 points that W. Edwards Deming employed in his work with postwar Japanese industries and that have been credited with turning around that once inefficient and backward economy. Basically, TQM is built on a set of core beliefs that boil down to:

1. The customer is the ultimate assessor of quality.
2. The goal of any quality-oriented enterprise is continuous improvement.
3. Continuous improvement follows when one knows who the customer is and what the customer's needs are, and one is willing to manifest a commitment to monitor and adjust the production process to ensure that the customer continues to receive a better product.

In education the most important customers are the students. It is they who will stagnate or develop as a consequence of participation in the instructional programs. The "taught curriculum" and the instructional practices make up the production process in schools, and the effective principal is in the best position to help a faculty monitor and adjust their approach to curriculum and instruction. Ultimately, effective administrative leadership provides the best leverage to produce performance gains for the customers (students).

That is why students of Deming and students of effective schools should not be surprised to find that both bodies of literature have concluded that excellent performance will occur only when and where leadership simultaneously provides focus, pressure, and support for those working in the enterprise. The phrase educators have used to describe this type of effective principal is the "instructional leader." Unfortunately, up until now those involved have done little but write case studies and call for more instructional leadership. Lacking has been a framework or a model that makes it clear what instructional leaders do for their organizations. This book is an attempt to put some flesh on the bones of an instructional leadership model that will come to characterize a new phenomenon in our schools—Total Quality Education (TQE). We have done this by using the nine attributes of successful leadership outlined by Deming as our framework and then offering the reader a variety of specific examples of these attributes as displayed by instructional leaders working in public schools.

Deming argued that effective leaders have these attributes:

1. They understand how the work of their group fits into the aims of the company.
2. They work with preceding stages and with following stages.
3. They try to create for everybody joy in work. They try to optimize the education, skills, and abilities of everyone and to help everyone improve.
4. They are coaches and counselors, not judges.
5. They use figures to help them understand their people and themselves. They understand variation. They use statistical calculation to learn who, if anybody, is outside the system, in need of special help.
6. They work to improve the system in which they and their people work.
7. They create trust.
8. They do not expect perfection.
9. They listen and learn.

In the pages that follow we will discuss these nine attributes in what we hope is a logical and systematic way. Occasionally we use synonyms and educational terminology in place of Deming's words, but we have endeavored to address each of the nine attributes as it relates to the instructional leadership function of the principal.

We begin in chapter 1 by looking at how leaders get a diverse faculty to pull together in pursuit of a collective vision. This is accomplished by examining a proven method for generating and gaining commitment to a shared vision: the *strategic planning* process.

Chapter 2 brings the key concepts of TQM right into the modern schoolhouse by asking the key questions: Who is the customer, and how can principals organize the suppliers (the faculty and staff) to maintain a focus on quality and continuous improvement? Chapter 3 addresses the role of instructional leader as "people developer." Deming has repeatedly pointed out that in terms of organizational effectiveness, people are not the problem (rather, the system is), but people should be part of the solution, for they are the ones who can both understand and alter the system. It is for this reason that a principal who wants to be a leader in the TQE tradition must be committed to optimizing the talents of all staff members. We discuss these issues in chapter 3 by outlining what is known about adult learning, organizational culture, and the cultivation of teacher leadership.

Chapter 4 builds on this foundation by offering concrete examples and specific suggestions for using peer coaching and peer supervision as mechanisms to foster continuous improvement. We shift gears in chapter 5, where we examine an essential feature of the TQM model—data-based decision making—and explore how a principal can help make this happen. This chapter details processes that have helped bring the visions created during strategic planning to fruition. Specifically, we discuss the use of *collaborative action research* and other mechanisms that have helped faculties align resources to priorities. We pay particular attention to the resource that matters the most and, yet, is most limited in schools: time.

Chapter 6 pulls together many of the pieces from chapters 1 through 5. In this chapter we focus on several mechanisms used by principals to build a professional learning community. Here we give practical advice on how to implement *management by walking around* (MBWA) in schools, how to use governance processes to maximum benefit, and what differentiates the leaders of learning communities from administrators in schools that appear to be "stuck." The book concludes with chapter 7, which presents an integrated model of the TQE instructional leadership process.

Our approach in this volume reflects several key assumptions we made about its use. We wanted the book to be helpful to incumbents in the principalship as well as to those aspiring to it. We wanted the book to be faithful to both TQM theory and current educational research, but we did not want it to be a theoretical text. Rather, we wanted to use theory sparingly and only as a framework on which we could build models through the use of concrete examples of practices that have proved successful for transformational school leaders.

The book is short. This, too, was deliberate. We never intended this book to be comprehensive. Rather, our hope was to stock these pages with starter ideas from which creative practitioners could craft their own solutions, appropriate to their own local contexts. Each chapter contains a discussion, examples of strategies, a glossary of key terms and concepts, and some references for those wishing to engage in further study.

Our goal for this book was to accomplish two things. First, we wanted to provide some beginning guidance to practitioners who wanted to apply the principles of Total Quality Education to the organizational challenges faced by their schools. Second, we wanted to make the point not only that leadership is an important ingredient if schools are to prosper, but that the need for quality instructional leadership is no less than a management imperative. If this book serves to inspire current and future school principals to energetically and creatively pursue school improvement through the application of their instructional leadership, we will feel that our mission was accomplished.

Richard Sagor
Washington State University

Bruce G. Barnett
University of Northern Colorado

About the Authors

Richard Sagor (Ph.D.) has 16 years of public school experience, including work as a classroom teacher, assistant superintendent, high school principal, instruction vice-principal, disciplinary vice-principal, and alternative school head teacher. He received his bachelor's degree from New York University and two master's degrees (in teaching disadvantaged youth and in juvenile corrections) and a doctorate in curriculum and instruction from the University of Oregon. While working as a teacher and administrator, he served as a site visitor for the U.S. Department of Education's Secondary School Recognition Program and as a consultant to numerous state departments of education and local school districts on leadership, effective schooling, student motivation, and teaching at-risk youth. He has authored many articles on education and school reform. "Perhaps the Nation Is At-Risk After All" received the Best Article by a Practitioner Award from the National Association of Secondary School Principals. His article "Discouraged Learners: Teetering on the Brink of Failure" won the Best Feature Award from the Educational Press Association of America. He recently authored *At-Risk Youth: Reaching and Teaching Them*.

Dr. Sagor is currently on the faculty of Washington State University, serving at the branch campus in Vancouver, Washington, where he directs several projects in collaboration with local schools. He is the coordinator of the Collaborative Professional Development Schools, a joint venture with several local school districts that emphasizes the development of educators as reflective practitioners and the creation of effective programs to serve at-risk youth. For 4 years he has directed Project LEARN (League of Educational Action Researchers in the Northwest), a consortium of schools and districts committed to school improvement fostered through the collaborative work of the professional staff. The techniques pioneered by Project LEARN are described in detail in his most recent book, *How to Conduct Collaborative Action Research*.

Bruce G. Barnett (Ph.D.) is an Associate Professor in the Division of Educational Leadership and Policy Studies at the University of Northern Colorado (UNC). Prior to joining the UNC faculty in the fall of 1990, he was a professor at Indiana University, where he focused on the preparation of educational leaders. Before entering higher education in 1987, he worked at the Far West Laboratory for Educational Research and Development, where he conducted classroom- and school-level research, developed and implemented a variety of workshops, and directed the Peer-Assisted Leadership program, a peer coaching program for school administrators. During his tenure at UNC, he has helped to create and deliver leadership preparation programs at the master's, certification, and doctoral levels. The development of educational platforms, the creation of portfolios, and the incorporation of cohort group learning are particular areas he is emphasizing in these preparation programs. His scholarly interests and writings focus on such issues as educational leadership preparation, instructional leadership, peer coaching, mentoring, reflective practice, and moral and ethical dimensions of school leadership.

✦ 1 ✦

Understanding How the Work of Groups Fits Into the School's Vision

How many times have we heard teachers and staff members remark:

"This is a completely different direction than last year. Whatever happened to the ideas we started last year?"

"They keep changing the focus. One year it's reading, the next year higher order thinking skills. What will they think up next year?"

"By this time next year we won't even be talking about cooperative learning. If we wait long enough, this will go away and so will the principal."

These comments reflect the frustration experienced by many teachers in schools today because they do not sense there is any rhyme or reason why new programs are created and quickly abandoned. Furthermore, they do not see any continuity or connection between what is being done now, what has been done in the past, and how this relates to where the school ought to be headed. This pattern of constantly trying to find the next great innovation to address the school's latest problem persists as a way of doing business in many districts and individual schools across the country. How often have educators been accused of "jumping on the next bandwagon" to solve an immediate problem?

This situation creates a dilemma for most school leaders, especially principals who are striving to provide instructional leadership in their buildings. On one hand, they feel the need to respond immediately and swiftly to the desires of different stakeholders in the educational process. On the other hand, principals want to provide the best educational experience possible for students in their schools. How then can principals "stick to the knitting" of schools as learning institutions given the increasing demands being placed on them from a variety of fronts?

W. Edwards Deming, the founding father of the TQM movement, contends his philosophy provides a solution to this problem. In particular, he advocates that leaders must constantly help other people in the organization make the connection between their individual and collective efforts and the ultimate purpose(s) of the organization. Although there are a multitude of approaches to accomplish this aim, this chapter discusses two ways for instructional leaders to create this sense of connection and purpose:

- Engaging teachers and staff members in a systematic *strategic planning* process
- Collaboratively involving staff members in developing a *vision* for the organization

The Strategic Planning Process

In recent years, many school districts and individual schools have embraced the strategic planning process. The basic premise behind this process is to involve a variety of people in deciding what the aims of school should be and how best to design and implement strategies to accomplish these aims.

Rather than simply being a planning process, strategic planning is meant to create results-based, action-oriented plans that can be implemented, measured, and refined over a 3- to 5-year time frame (Burrello & Associates, 1989). Such an approach is precisely the type of thinking advanced by TQM. Because it is systematic and ongoing, strategic planning can assist school leaders and teachers in making informed decisions about how to commit resources toward established goals and priorities.

Steps in the Strategic Planning Process

There are various strategic planning models in operation; however, a common set of sequential steps or phases composes most of these models:

1. Beliefs and values: A statement of the underlying beliefs, values, and convictions of people in the organization.
2. Mission: A statement of the purpose of the organization and the function(s) it performs.
3. External and internal analysis: The social, political, economic, and human factors that influence the school's operation.
4. Essential policies: The set of norms that guide people's actions, especially in achieving the overall purpose or aim of the organization.
5. Objectives: The specific and measurable results needed to achieve the mission.
6. Strategies: The ways in which resources are deployed to achieve each objective.
7. Action plans: A detailed description of the tasks required to implement the desired strategies.
8. Review and recycle: A system for monitoring and adjusting the decisions and plans as they are implemented.

A common approach when implementing the strategic planning process is to establish a *planning team* and a series of *action teams*, one for each strategy. A planning team consists of 25 to 30 people from the community and the schools whose job is to: (a) complete phases 1 through 6 of the process (beliefs and values through strategies), (b) create action teams to prepare the action plans (phase 7), and (c) to monitor plans and their implementation (phase 8). The action teams are composed of at least one member of the planning team and four or five other people whose particular interests and backgrounds are suited to the strategy they are undertaking. Action teams develop and submit their plans to the planning team, adjusting their plans based on the reactions and suggestions of the planning team. Action teams are not required to actually conduct the plans they develop; however, enough detail should be provided for those people who finally are entrusted to implement the plan.

Planning team members require a concentrated period of time to complete the first six phases. Although some schools try to devote 2 or 3 hours at a time for this planning, it may be preferable to allow the planning team to complete its initial work during a 2- or 3-day retreat. Devoting this period of continuous time allows group members to build norms and to focus all of their attention on the tasks at hand. Subsequent meetings of the planning team and the action teams can be handled during 2- or 3-hour time periods.

Principals who have not participated in such a strategic planning process might wonder what the products for each of these phases might look like. Listed next is additional clarification of the elements to consider within each phase, followed by examples of actual products that have been created.

Beliefs. Articulating the organization's convictions, values, and ethics provides precise, formal statements of what the organization aspires to be. As a starting point, these values are important because they provide: (a) the value system on which the strategic plan must be built and (b) a public declaration of what the organization stands for. These statements should be brief and precise. Belief statements might read as follows:

- We believe learning is a lifelong process.
- We believe positive self-image facilitates learning.
- We believe students have a right to a safe, comfortable, and secure learning environment.
- We believe schools should address the physical, emotional, academic, and social needs of students.
- We believe teachers should be involved in making collective decisions and being accountable for results.

Mission. Schools need to clearly state why they exist. Thus a mission is a rather broad statement of the purpose for which the organization exists (Nanus, 1992) and can be distinguished from its vision, or direction (which is addressed later in this chapter). When creating a *mission statement*, these "three A's" should be considered:

- The *aim* or outcome that is desired
- The *actions* or behaviors to be engaged in
- The *audience* or clients being affected

Each of the following sample mission statements pays attention to these components:

> Our mission is to prepare all students to become lifelong learners who are self-supporting, responsible, participating members of American and world societies. (San Diego City Schools)

> Our mission is to provide effective instruction in basic skills, to develop the potential of all students, to nurture a sense of individual worth, and to build a foundation for lifelong learning in a changing world. The district, in partnership with the community, is committed to serve all students with academic, cultural, vocational, and activity programs that meet the highest standards of educational excellence. (School district in Iowa)

> Our mission is to provide a stimulating educational environment to prepare individuals for lifelong learning and for becoming responsible citizens in an ever-changing world. (School district in Indiana)

External and internal analysis. This level of analysis is meant to determine what external conditions will be impacting the school in the next 3 to 5 years as well as the existing strengths and weaknesses of the organization. By better understanding the external and internal environments and how they contribute to or inhibit the organization's mission, people are in a position to reach their desired goals by utilizing their current strengths and acknowledging their inherent weaknesses. The importance of such analyses will be further examined in chapter 2 when we discuss the forces impinging on the school organization. An external analysis would include examining social, political, demographic, economic, technological, and educational trends. An illustration of an external analysis might reveal:

Factor	*Impact*
Population decline	Reduction in state funds
	Reduction in school programs
Increase in single-parent families	Reduced income per household
	Less parental involvement in school activities
	Greater need for social services for families
Unemployment increase	More dependency on state welfare system
	Increase in crime
	Less money for community development
Increase in home schooling	Increased competition
	Reduction in state funds
	Fewer parents in the workforce

Likewise, an internal analysis might uncover the following strengths and weaknesses:

Strengths	*Weaknesses*
Child-centered staff	Curriculum not articulated across grades
Community is supportive	Apathy of veteran teachers
Student achievement is increasing	Evaluation plan is cumbersome
Efficient internal communication	Nonsupportive local media
Businesses provide grants	School board is factionalized

Essential policies. Another aid to making decisions is the creation of a set of guidelines or parameters to determine appropriate actions. These guidelines become the working norms of the organization rather than formal board policies or statements of standard operating procedures. Typically, these essential policies dictate what will not be tolerated in reaching the mission. Examples of essential policies might include:

- We will not accept a new program unless: a favorable cost-benefit analysis has been performed; a provision for staff development is included; an evaluation plan is incorporated.
- We will not allow any actions to degrade or restrict the rights of individual students or teachers.
- We will not forget that our educational community is a team of parents, educators, students, and patrons sharing responsibility and acting cooperatively for common goals.
- No curricular program will be sacrificed based solely on economics.

Objectives. At this stage in the process, attention is given to developing a series of specific, measurable results, especially ones that demonstrate a commitment to achieving the mission statement while remaining true to the underlying beliefs. Whereas a mission is a broad and general statement of the purpose of the organization, objectives are time bound and are measurable in terms of the time and money required for their completion, the quality of the end result, or the quantity of what will be produced. Those who advocate this level of specificity for objectives contend that without measurable results schools will not know if they are achieving their desired outcomes. Examples of objectives include:

- To increase parental involvement in each school's decision-making process by June 1, 1994
- To make counseling services available to all students by August 30, 1994
- To achieve a more balanced class size distribution in elementary, junior high, and high school classrooms by August 30, 1995

Strategies. In order to accomplish each objective, a series of actions and events are prescribed. In essence, these strategies are how the organization will work to reach each objective by committing the needed physical, financial, and human resources. Listed next are strategies for an objective dealing with expanding counseling services.

Objective: To expand the counseling services to meet the needs of all students by September 1, 1995.

Strategies for 1993-94:

1. We will add one elementary school guidance counselor.
2. We will add one junior high school guidance counselor.
3. We will retain the current K-12 at-risk counselor.

Strategies for 1994-95:

1. We will add one senior high school guidance counselor.
2. We will survey students and teachers to determine the quality of counseling services.
3. We will request additional funding from state and federal agencies to support existing programs.

Action plans. At this point in the process, the planning team establishes a series of action teams, each of which is responsible for developing operational plans for one or more of the strategies. Each team outlines the required tasks, prepares a timeline, and estimates the resources needed to successfully implement the strategy. Although action teams are not charged with actually conducting the plans they create, they may specify who should be involved and how the tasks might be completed. Here is an example of an action plan:

Strategy: We will design a districtwide public relations marketing system.

Tasks	Timeline	Cost	Responsibility
Gather data about other schools	10/93-12/93	$0	Asst. Superintendent
Gather census data	10/93-12/93	$0	Asst. Superintendent
Conduct telephone survey	1/94-3/94	$50	Communications Dept.
Consult public relations firms	10/93-2/94	$0	Communications Dept.
Design/complete brochure	3/94-4/94	$1,000	Communications Dept.
Create newspaper ads	4/94	$50	Communications Dept.
Conduct follow-up survey	10/94	$50	Communications Dept.
Summarize survey data	11/94	$0	Communications Dept.
Formalize marketing plan	1/95	$0	Asst. Superintendent, Communications Dept.

Review and recycle. In order to monitor the progress and to adjust the planning process, the planning team acts as a governing body. Their role is to review each action team's plans and to provide suggestions for improving the planning process. In addition, as new needs and interests develop, their job is to revisit the first six phases of the process to determine if changes are warranted, especially in creating new objectives and strategies. In this way, the process regenerates itself, rather than being stagnant and nonresponsive to new demands.

Developing Successful Work Teams

For the strategic planning process to succeed, a collective effort among a variety of constituencies is required. Therefore, principals must be able to muster the support and involvement of the teaching staff, parents, and local community. A TQM environment is characterized by all members of the work team feeling as though they are contributing to the decision-making process. Recent evidence suggests there are a variety of features or qualities that characterize successful work teams. For example, the findings of Larson and LaFasto (1992) provide helpful guidelines for principals who are using planning and action teams as part of the strategic planning process:

- Have a vision for what should or could be, enact change, and unleash the talents and energy of the team members.
- Make sure the team's goal is clearly specified, is personally challenging, and creates a sense of urgency.
- Help team members to establish clear roles and accountabilities, to create a system where individual performance is monitored and feedback is provided, and to use objective and factual information in making decisions.
- Select team members who possess the necessary technical skills, motivation to contribute to the task, and ability to collaborate, and who are dedicated to spending their personal time and energy to successfully complete the task.
- Assist team members in developing mutual trust so they can remain focused on the problem, use their time more efficiently, develop open lines of communication, and take over for one another when necessary.
- Provide teams with adequate human and material resources and publicly recognize their accomplishments.

Creating a Shared Vision

Although the strategic planning process is a systematic way for principals to link goals, objectives, and actions, it can be an extremely lengthy and time-consuming process. A potentially less cumbersome approach in helping people to connect their daily actions with the goals, aims, or direction of the organization is to use a *visioning process*. Visions are a desirable future state of the organization and are intended to inspire and energize people.

There is a growing belief in education that by having a vigorous and shared image of what a school should be like, school reform can be better focused and coordinated. To Roland Barth (1993) a vision is:

> ... a kind of moral imagination which gives school people, individually and collectively, the ability to see their school not only as it is, but as they would like it to become. It is an overall conception of what educators want their school to stand for, a map revealing how all the parts fit together, and above all how the vision of each individual is related to the collective vision of the organization. (p. 10)

Often visions and missions are viewed interchangeably; however, Burt Nanus (1992) contends there are some important distinctions:

- A mission predicts the future; a vision is not necessarily a prophecy of what will definitely happen.
- A mission specifies an organization's purpose and function; a vision clarifies its direction.
- A mission is meant to be achieved; a vision may never be realized as originally stated.
- A mission focuses attention in a certain direction; a vision stimulates opportunities and is a catalyst for action.

Tom Peters (1987) in his book *Thriving on Chaos* suggests that visions are a way to prepare for the future by honoring what has worked successfully in the past. The real value of visions, and why they are important to an instructional leader, is his contention that visions help people in the organization make sense of their actions. Similarly, Joel Barker (1990), a self-described futurist who works with business corporations interested in change, believes that every decision needs to be measured against the vision and each person must understand how his or her actions relate to the vision. Although Peters and Barker work primarily with business organizations, their ideas are relevant to schools, principals, and teachers.

Engaging in the Visioning Process

To an instructional leader, being visionary or engaging in the visioning process may appear to be somewhat nebulous and ill defined. How can an instructional leader assist other people in creating a vision and help them to determine how their daily actions are achieving this desired future state? There clearly are different ways to create visions, from refining the current vision to borrowing a new vision to hiring a person with a vision (Barth, 1993). Although there is no magic formula for visioning, there are three practical approaches—systematic vision development, vision statements, and educational platforms—that can assist instructional leaders and other people in the organization to clarify the school's direction and to connect members' actions with desired outcomes.

Systematic vision development. Nanus (1992) describes a four-phase process of visioning that allows members of an organization to create a vision. The process begins with an investigation of the way the organization currently operates and concludes with a way to articulate the vision to members of the organization and the community. This approach is similar in some ways to the strategic planning process because there is a seemingly rational, step-by-step approach to creating a vision. The difference is that this systematic visioning strategy outlines a series of questions that need to be answered and does not specify an organizational structure for how to accomplish the visioning process. The four phases of this vision development process include:

1. The vision audit: Examine the nature of the organization, how it operates, and its current direction.
2. The vision scope: Determine the constituencies served by the organization, potential barriers to the vision, and how the vision might appear in practice.
3. The vision context: Anticipate the important future developments and the probability of their occurrence.
4. The vision choice: Select the correct vision and package it.

Once a vision is selected using this process, an instructional leader needs to translate the vision into the everyday routines of the organization. This occurs by being a spokesperson for the vision, being an active change agent, coaching others in the implementation of the vision, monitoring the progress made toward the vision, and developing the capacity of others to lead the organization toward its vision.

Vision statements. The visioning process described previously can be lengthy and time-consuming, similar to strategic planning. A more practical and tangible way that leaders can assist other people in visioning is to help them to literally "sense" what will be happening when they are successfully achieving a desired outcome. Using their sensory modalities, such as sight and sound, allows people to envision what will be happening as a goal is realized. This visualization technique has been used effectively with athletes as they prepare for a competition. By "seeing" themselves being successful in a swimming event, cross-country race, or basketball game, athletes can become inspired and committed to achieve at a higher level of performance.

In educational settings, instructional leaders can assist other people in creating vision statements aimed at different personal or organizational goals or objectives. Following are examples of vision statements that might be created for particular goals.

Goal	Vision Statement
1. To increase student attendance	In the lounge, several teachers are enthusiastically discussing the lead article in the school newspaper titled, "School attendance figures reach a 5-year high."
2. To improve the school's discipline	The assistant principal and I smile and raise our clenched fists when the secretary tells us that no students have been sent to the office for fighting for the second straight week.

3. To create a successful learning environment for all children

As the superintendent enters my office, she seems pleased that our test scores have improved. She says that members of the school board reported hearing many compliments from parents about the quality of the instructional program, especially for non-English-speaking students.

As these examples demonstrate, vision statements indicate what might happen if goals are being achieved. In some cases, inferences are provided (e.g., enthusiastically discussing, seems pleased) while in other instances behavioral indicators are used (e.g., hands folded, raise our clenched fists). As a general rule, the more specific these statements are written using exact quotes, behaviors, and physical gestures, the better people are able to visualize the situation. Because decisions in a TQM organization must be data driven (see chapter 5), creating such images not only helps people to anticipate what might occur when successfully reaching a goal, but also sensitizes them to what to look for as they are engaged in the change process. All too often as new approaches and strategies are introduced, whether the desired effects are being realized is forgotten. Vision statements can keep people focused on what things will look and feel like as they are immersed in the daily tasks and activities of school renewal.

Educational platforms. One clear message in the literature on visions is that each individual must understand how his or her actions contribute to the accomplishment of the vision. The challenge for instructional leaders, therefore, is to provide opportunities for other people to articulate their own value systems and determine how their personal visions are consistent with or are incompatible with the overall vision of the school. One way to assist teachers and staff members in revealing their beliefs and values is to have them prepare an educational platform. Simply stated, an educational platform is a person's philosophy of education. Although there is not a predetermined set of issues that every platform should address, there are some general suggestions of areas to include, such as the aims of education, important student outcomes, preferred teaching strategies and climate, and desired school-community relations (e.g., Barnett, 1991; Sergiovanni & Starratt, 1984).

Educational platforms can be used to assist teachers in comparing their personal beliefs and actions with the direction or vision of the school. Principals can ask each teacher to prepare an individual platform focusing on several key issues, such as desirable student outcomes and the type of climate and instructional strategies needed to achieve these outcomes. Figure 1.1 provides a format that teachers can use to create their platforms. The advantage of using such a format is that everyone is focusing on the same types of issues, allowing for the development of common language and understanding. This format has been used with teachers and principals to develop their educational platforms; our experience suggests all levels of educational professionals can use this generic model when contemplating the factors that influence their roles.

One value of having all the teaching staff create platforms is that they will begin to clarify the particular standards they wish to see occurring in the school. In particular, platforms can assist a teaching staff to determine:

- Standards for their own personal behavior
- Standards for other educators and the educational system
- Standards for students
- Standards for parents and the community
- Standards for the learning environment

Using the format suggested in Figure 1.1, instructional leaders can facilitate collective discussions by having teachers compare their platforms by grade levels or disciplines, noting areas of commonality or disagreement about these different standards. As a result of discussing their philosophies, they are more likely to reach some consensus on where the school should be headed (student outcomes), how the curricular content and instructional

16 ✧ The TQE Principal: A Transformed Leader

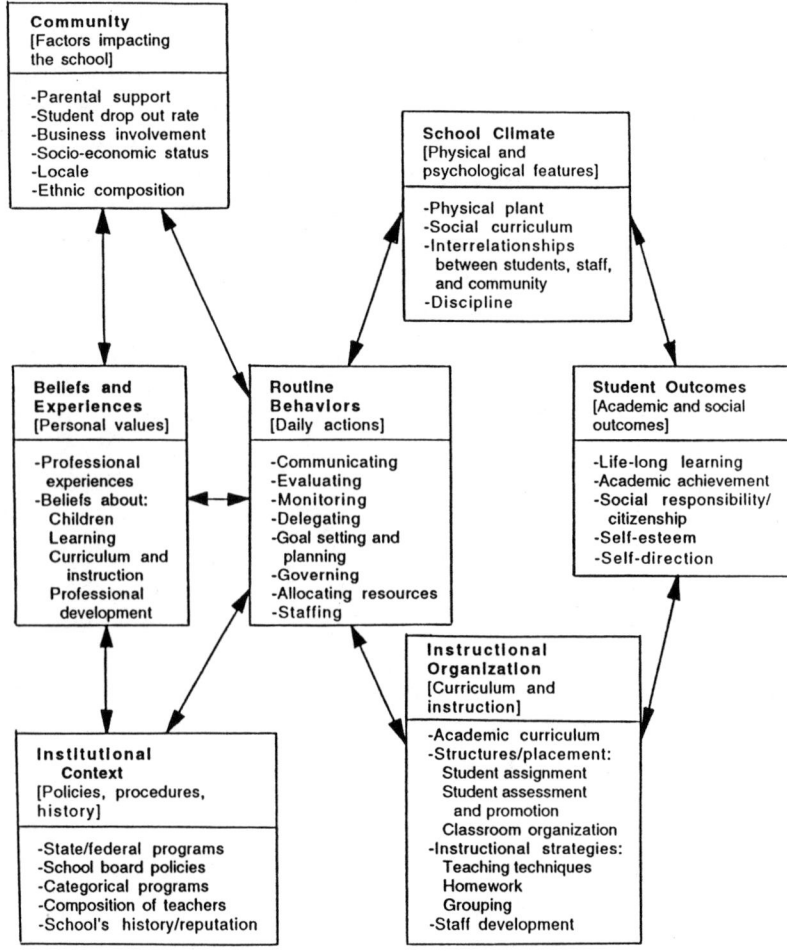

Figure 1.1. Examples of Features Addressed in an Educational Platform

strategies (instructional climate, instructional organization) can support their collective vision, and how external forces support or inhibit their efforts (community, institutional context). Eventually, teachers can develop a collective platform that synthesizes the ideas of each person's platform, which then becomes the overall vision and the working parts needed to achieve the vision.

There are several advantages to using a common format for platform development, especially one that can be represented visually:

- Teachers can begin to "see" how different parts of the system influence where the school is headed.
- If staff members have created personal versions of the platform, they are better able to see how their actions fit in and influence the school's direction.
- The visual representation becomes a framework for understanding how future programs, actions, and policies can support where the school is going.
- Instructional leaders and teachers can constantly use this composite platform to monitor their current actions, checking to see how or if their daily routines are fitting into the aim of the organization.

Overall, this framework stimulates *systemic thinking*, an important feature of TQE that will be further elaborated on in the next chapter.

In sum, the hectic daily events of schools often prohibit principals and teachers from concentrating on the goals of the school or where the school is ultimately headed. Just to get through the day without any major catastrophes can be quite an accomplishment. Unfortunately, without any sense of shared purpose, teachers can feel quite isolated and not believe their efforts are contributing to the overall success of the school. To create a collective sense of purpose and accomplishment, the effective instructional leader must engage the teaching staff in different kinds of discussions and activities than normally occur. Engaging in a strategic planning process, creating vision statements, and developing and sharing educational platforms all are active ways in which principals can engage teachers in discussions that demonstrate how the daily actions of both groups are contributing to the overall purpose of the school organization.

Key Terms and Concepts

Action team. A group of people who are part of the strategic planning process. Their role is to develop specific plans and activities aimed at accomplishing an objective and to submit these to the planning team for their review.

Characteristics of successful work teams. For members of a work team to succeed, they need to have a clear and elevating goal, communicate effectively, possess the necessary technical skills, be dedicated to accomplishing the task, be able to collaborate, trust other members of the group, be adequately recognized for their efforts, and have a leader who is willing to unleash the talents and energy of the team.

Educational platform. A person's espoused beliefs and values about education. This can be a formally prepared document that can be shared and discussed with other professional educators.

External and internal analyses. A phase in the strategic planning process during which external forces (e.g., political climate, demographic changes) and internal forces (e.g., teaching staff, professional development resources) are critically examined to determine how they are affecting the school's mission.

Mission statement. A statement summarizing the purpose of a school or organization. The statement should include the aims of the organization, the audience served, and the actions taken to achieve the aims.

Planning team. A group of school and community members who oversees the strategic planning process. This group not only develops pieces of the strategic plan, but also oversees the implementation and refinement of the plan.

Strategic planning. A systematic process for developing a direction or mission for a school or district and for determining the policies, the human and fiscal resources, and the activities needed to successfully achieve the desired mission.

Vision. A desirable future state that a school organization aspires to reach.

Vision statements. Written or verbal statements that demonstrate in detail what people will be doing, feeling, and/or experiencing when they are successfully accomplishing a goal. This visualization technique often has been used in preparing athletes for athletic competition.

References

Barker, J. R. (1990). *The power of vision* [Videotape]. Barnsville, MN: Charthouse International.

Barnett, B. G. (1991). The educational platform: Articulating moral dilemmas and choices for future educational leaders. In B. G. Barnett, F. O. McQuarrie, & C. J. Norris (Eds.), *The moral imperatives of leadership: A focus on human decency* (pp. 129-153). Fairfax, VA: National Policy Board for Educational Administration.

Barth, R. S. (1993). Coming to a vision. *Journal of Staff Development, 14,* 6-11.

Burrello, L. C., & Associates. (1989). *LEAD strategic planning process.* Bloomington: Indiana University.

Larson, C. E., & LaFasto, F. M. J. (1992). *Teamwork: What must go right/what can go wrong.* Newbury Park, CA: Sage.

Nanus, B. (1992). *Visionary leadership: Creating a compelling sense of direction for your organization.* San Francisco: Jossey-Bass.

Peters, T. (1987). *Thriving on chaos.* New York: Random House.

Sergiovanni, T. J., & Starratt, R. (1984). *Supervision: Human perspectives.* New York: McGraw-Hill.

✧ 2 ✧

Involving Both "Customers" and "Suppliers" for Improved Outcomes

For years educational leaders have discussed the importance of being proactive rather than reactive. Most experienced administrators agree that if a leader allows the momentary flow of events to dictate the course of action to take, rather than being guided by a clear vision of where the organization needs to be headed, then the organization will never get where it should be. The merit of being a vision-driven leader may seem obvious (as much of the material in the previous chapter illustrates). But is being a proactive agent in pursuit of a vision sufficient? In other words, is the resolute pursuit of a vision enough of a navigation strategy to successfully guide an organization as complex as a modern public school?

TQM advocates like Deming as well as Peter Senge (1990) and his associates at MIT's Sloan School of Management argue that there may be another critical element in organizational leadership that is even more important than vision and proaction—*systemic thinking*. What precisely is meant by systemic thinking?

Systemic thinking is the perspective taken by a leader when viewing a problem that takes into account the preceding stages, the work process, and the outcomes to be obtained. By engaging in systemic thinking the leader provides "super-vision" over the full range of interactions that make up a chain of events (Sergiovanni & Starratt, 1993). As a result, the skilled systemic thinker is unlikely to place an inordinate amount of responsibility or blame on any one feature of a process, but is more likely to believe that the performance of the organization is a consequence of a set of processes that are working in harmony or disharmony. The format for preparing an educational platform (see Figure 1.1) is one way to visually represent many of the antecedents, processes, and outcomes.

As Figure 1.1 suggests, there is an array of factors that can contribute to a child learning or not learning the school curriculum. The child's predisposition regarding course content, the child's prior history with the teacher, and the school's hidden curriculum are a few of these. Furthermore, the appropriateness of available instructional materials and the teaching techniques employed by the child's teacher, the prerequisite skills brought by the student, and the pedagogical skill of the teacher will have an influence on the ultimate outcomes obtained. The principal who wishes to foster improved learning must look at each one of these factors and the way they interrelate, rather than simply staking out a proactive position, for example, choosing to implement a new teacher evaluation system or adopting a new "improved" curriculum.

The most dramatic change that systemic thinking creates for a classically trained school leader is a refocusing of concern away from the performance problems of individual personnel to an analysis of systemic factors. Deming (1986) has asserted that 85% of an organization's problems are systemic, whereas the employees account for only 15% of performance variance. By accepting this perspective it becomes clear that the job of the instructional leader needs to shift. The systemic principal's new role becomes one of learning how to motivate employees to change their system rather than to change themselves. We will return to specific ways to do this a little later.

What We Know About Change in School Settings

There is voluminous literature regarding change in schools (Berman & McLaughlin, 1974; Corbett, Dawson, & Firestone, 1984;

Fullan & Stiegelbauer, 1991). These and other studies explore the key variables that need to be considered, the obstacles that will likely be encountered, and the motivational needs of professional school employees who are attempting improvements. For this discussion neither is it necessary nor is there enough space to review all of the change studies; however, two points are crucial:

1. Change is a personal experience.
2. People must change first; only then can their institutions be expected to change. (Hall & Hord, 1987)

How can this relate to the work of principals as instructional leaders? First, as Deming suggests, certain behaviors such as preaching to the group, evoking slogans, and using elaborate financial incentives probably will not prove to be among the most effective ways to inspire change with professional employees. Instead the effective instructional leader needs to find ways to reconstruct the system so that each individual worker can find "joy in the enterprise." Once a system is designed in which each worker is finding satisfaction in his or her work, is developing a commitment to a collective vision, and is feeling an allegiance to the institution, then the stage is set for real change.

Later in this chapter several techniques will be suggested that can assist a principal in engaging in meaningful systemic intervention with individual teachers. But first we will consider how the dynamics of group process work in schools by looking at what makes for a successful work group.

What Makes for a Functional School Work Group?

Earlier in chapter 1 we noted important features that instructional leaders should attend to when creating work teams. Furthermore, motivation theory indicates that adults in the workplace are primarily motivated to satisfy one of three emotional needs: (a) power, (b) achievement, and (c) affiliation.

Although all three of these needs may be part of a person's individual makeup, one of the three needs will dominate the psychological landscape of each person. Many educational critics have missed the target with their reform strategies by assuming that teachers (and other school employees) are primarily achievement motivated. If teachers were, in fact, achievement motivated, then innovations such as merit pay would have attracted a popular following within the teaching corps. In fact, the reason for widespread faculty rejection of merit pay is that a high percentage of teachers tend to be affiliation motivated. Affiliation-motivated people derive their employment satisfaction and intrinsic rewards from the people with whom they work. Affiliation-motivated people tend to enjoy their interaction with colleagues and, therefore, intuitively reject motivational strategies that place them in competition with co-workers. The next chapter discusses how satisfying affiliation needs is one of the most powerful lessons to be learned from adult learning theory.

Power-motivated individuals are people who place a high priority on having personal control over their work environment. A significant number of power-motivated folks are found in education. After all, where else can a professional exercise more discretion? Once the classroom door shuts, teachers are on their own to structure the learning experience, the use of time, and the interaction of the children in whatever manner they feel best.

Putting these three pieces (systemic thinking, the change process, and motivation theory) together, we see the challenge for instructional leaders this way: Effective principals need to learn to view their enterprises through a systemic lens, they must take into account the personal aspects of the change process, and they need to operate from an understanding of the motivational issues that are played out in collaborative work groups. The rest of this chapter will explore strategies that effective principals have used to deliver on this challenge.

Who Is the Customer?

Two unifying themes of TQM are (a) that the *customer* is the one player in the best position to perceive quality and (b) that the goal of any production or service organization is, above all else, customer satisfaction. But one of the difficulties for leaders of complex enterprises, like public school principals, is to clearly determine at any point in time *who is the customer*.

When approaching leadership from a systemic perspective one looks at each aspect of the organization as having three stages: inputs, throughputs (or processes), and outputs. The customer is the person or group who consumes the output. So who is the customer of the public schools? The answer can vary depending on the subprocess being discussed. For example, the faculty is the consumer of staff development, the students are the consumers of student activities, and employers are the consumers of the graduates.

This is no small matter. Mistakes on customer identification can have serious ramifications for quality. For example, it is clear that the students/athletes are in the best position to judge the quality and adequacy of the school activities program, rather than their coaches; and the teachers are in a better position to assess the relevance of staff development than is their director of curriculum and instruction.

Creating a two-column customer diagnostic chart is a helpful strategy for people leading school improvement efforts. When using such a chart, the first task is to clearly state and record each desired outcome (e.g., improved literacy, responsibility, or knowledge of a mathematical operation) and write them in the left-hand column. Then for each identified outcome one needs to determine who most directly receives the benefit (the customer) and, therefore, who is in the best position to assess the quality of the service.

*Prioritizing Daily Activities
for the Customer's Advantage*

A technique that can prove helpful for instructional leaders wishing to spend their resources wisely is the *priority pie*. The priority pie is created by analyzing those elements in a system that contribute to its effectiveness and their relative importance by following a four-step process:

1. Individual brainstorming of all the significant factors that contribute to an outcome

2. Tentative assignment of "percentage of influence" for each factor
3. Sharing of individual lists
4. Arriving at a group consensus on the relative power of each factor

For example, assume that a faculty wants to examine the factors that they suspect are contributing to a school's instructional effectiveness. For the sake of this example assume also that this faculty agreed with the findings of the effective schooling research and concluded that six factors contributed most heavily to a school's effectiveness: (a) strong administrative leadership, (b) clarity of goals, (c) focus of resources on goals, (d) safe and orderly environment, (e) monitoring of student learning, and (f) high expectations (Edmonds, 1979).

After some discussion the faculty agreed to the following allocation of responsibility for the effectiveness outcome: (a) 33.0%, high expectations; (b) 8.5%, strong administrative leadership; (c) 33.0%, clarity of goals; (d) 8.5%, focus of resources on goals; (e) 8.5%, safe and orderly environment; and (f) 8.5%, monitoring of student learning.

Those weighted assignments of responsibility are then plotted into a pie chart using a protractor. A priority pie for school effectiveness would then look like Figure 2.1.

The value of a priority pie is the way it helps to allocate the most important resources at disposal (time and energy). If together the holding of high expectations and the focus on clear and unambiguous goals accounts for two thirds of a school's effectiveness, then it is reasonable (even imperative) that instructional leaders devote the majority of their time toward ensuring that these factors are in place and receiving adequate attention. If a school principal looked at a personal time log (time use is discussed later in this book; see chapter 5) and found that 60% of his or her time was spent responding to district requests for paperwork and budgetary management, while only 10% was devoted to issues that contributed to high shared expectations, then that principal ought not be surprised to find that the level of effectiveness being achieved at the school was below expectations. A priority pie analysis would help this principal see the discrepancy between expenditure of resource and organizational need.

26 ✧ The TQE Principal: A Transformed Leader

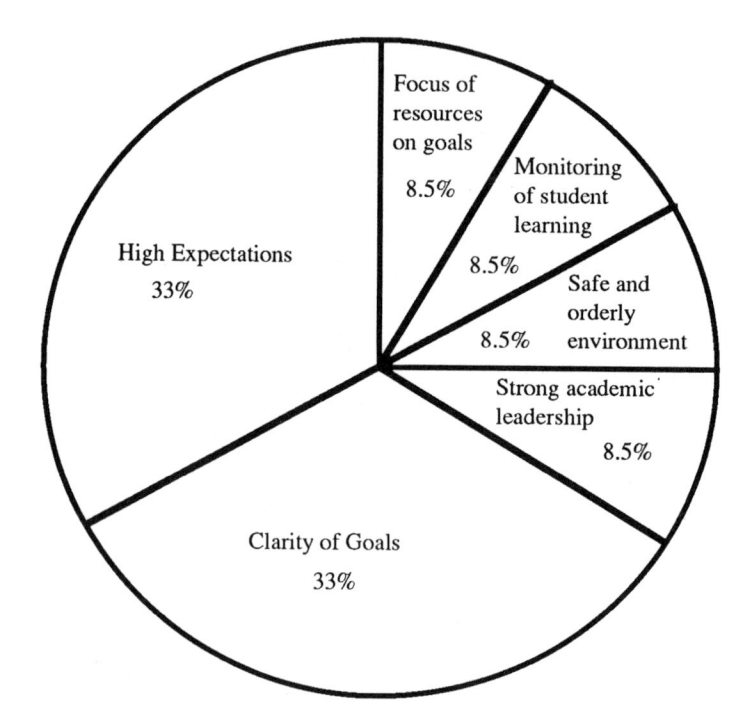

Figure 2.1. Priority Pie: School Effectiveness

- High Expectations 33%
- Focus of resources on goals 8.5%
- Monitoring of student learning 8.5%
- Safe and orderly environment 8.5%
- Strong academic leadership 8.5%
- Clarity of Goals 33%

To construct pies for each of the customers identified in the customer diagnostic charts requires being able to clearly state (a) who the customer is, (b) the needs sought by that customer, and (c) an assessment of what it will take to meet those needs.

Examples of customer-driven priority pies follow. Figure 2.2 examines the relative expectations of parent customers: (a) 25%, child safety; (b) 25%, social, emotional, and ethical development; (c) 33%, academic growth; and (d) 17%, having fun.

Figure 2.3 considers the expectations of corporate customers (employers): (a) 20%, job skills; (b) 50%, lifelong learning skills; and (c) 30%, personal habits, standards, and sense of responsibility.

Once priority pies have been developed it becomes the responsibility of both leadership and the "lead" to organize their work to see that effort corresponds to need. The final stage focusing on customer needs requires the direct involvement of the customers

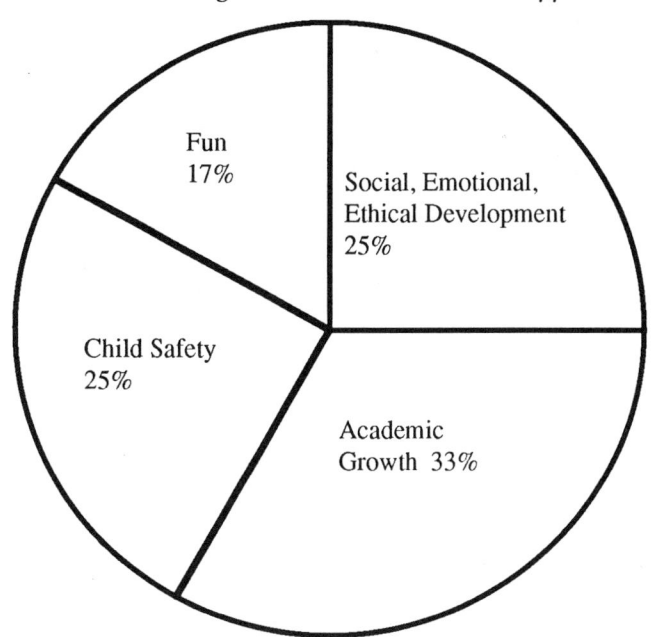

Figure 2.2. Priority Pie: Parents as Customers

themselves. This is where the leader shares with the customers the organization's understanding of their input and how their feedback was prioritized, and then asks the customers for feedback on how well leadership (the supplier) did in responding to the input. This is done by involving the customers in performance assessment.

Involving Customers in Assessment

Periodically organizations that have made quality their focus will ask their customers for feedback on how well they are succeeding at matching resources and effort with customer needs. There are several ways that a principal can organize a staff to do this. Although written surveys are the methods most often utilized for this purpose, a more powerful mechanism for soliciting this type of information is direct one-to-one communications that can later be aggregated for group analysis. For example, teachers might be asked to share the priority pies they have developed with

28 ✧ The TQE Principal: A Transformed Leader

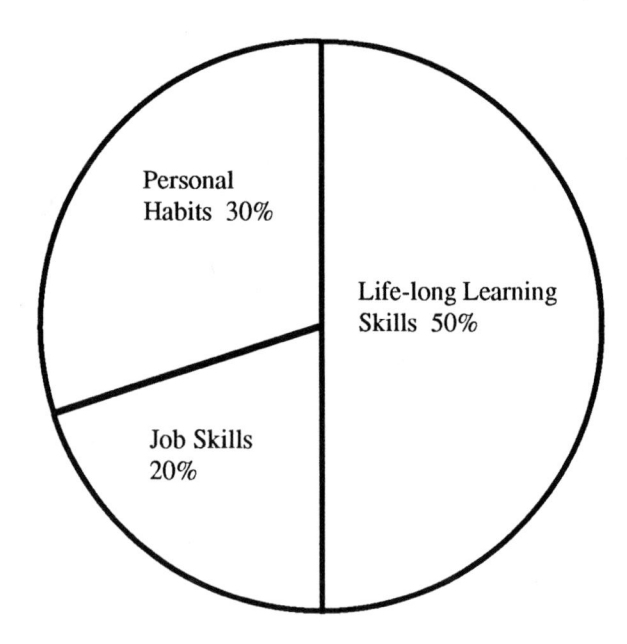

Figure 2.3. Priority Pie: Employers as Customers

parents during conferences and ask the parents to respond to these questions: Did you perceive our energies were spent in line with these priorities? With which priorities did you feel we were most effective? Which priorities do you feel should receive more of our emphasis and attention in the future?

Employers of recent graduates might be told specifically of the things that the school emphasized and then asked: Based on your experience with our students, did you perceive our energies were spent in line with these priorities? With which priorities did you feel we were effective? Which priorities do you feel should receive more emphasis and attention in the future?

The principal might share with the teachers a priority pie that captured the elements of leadership that he or she was attempting to provide and ask: Did you perceive my energies were spent in line with these priorities? With which priorities did you feel I was effective? Which priorities do you feel I should give more emphasis and attention to in the future?

Organizing the Suppliers

There is no one structure that makes sense for the organization of personnel in a school. However, it is clear that in a TQE school organizational patterns are chosen because of their potential to meet customer needs. For example, organizing secondary schools into departments or elementary schools into grade level teams may be functional for the customer group of faculty (it may make it easier for them to focus on common issues), but it may not be a logical organizational structure to meet the needs of parent, employer, and student customers. For instance, parents might be better served by having the suppliers organized into vertically integrated work groups. In such a structure each teacher might be more likely to be aware and concerned about systemic issues, particularly focusing on what went on before and what might be encountered next, in the student experience.

For this reason it will prove helpful to have multiple, flexible approaches to the arrangement of work groups and to constantly evaluate their effectiveness. But there are two other reasons for focusing on work group construction. First, faculties derive a great deal of their work satisfaction from the colleagues in their work groups. Second, work groups are the best vehicle for developing and sustaining an ethos of continuous improvement.

*Work Group Organization
to Foster Continuous Improvement*

A drive for continuous improvement can be enhanced by leadership's efforts to align behavior with expectations. Ultimately, an ethos of continuous improvement must become internalized if the school is to become a learning organization (Senge, 1990). The question for instructional leadership then becomes how a principal can orchestrate the continuous improvement ethic in the school. Although chapters 3, 4, and 6 will further examine this ethic, one proven method is the departmental and grade level improvement process (DIP and GLIP). Instructional leaders who have implemented these processes have done so by using a deliberate and sequential process involving these steps:

1. Producing readiness for continuous improvement
2. Providing successful experiences with continuous improvement
3. Institutionalizing the continuous improvement ethic

Step #1: Readiness. The TQE principal who wants the lead to take continuous progress to heart must become a partner with the teachers in carrying out the process. The mechanism for doing this is the "educational limited partnership." Although it may be too much to expect a principal to become totally engrossed in the improvement priorities of each individual teacher, it is not too much to expect the principal to emotionally join up with as many as 10 to 12 work groups, each of which has identified a priority project that can be expected to contribute to systemic improvement.

Principals have used a variety of techniques to succeed with step #1 (readiness). Some have required each department or grade level to generate an improvement plan of its own liking. Others have encouraged ad hoc groups to form, each of which is encouraged to create a written plan that targets growth and development. Whichever technique is utilized, the leader must be prepared to show encouragement and enthusiasm for the work group's effort.

Once publicly presented (presentation has been done in a number of ways), the principal becomes a "limited partner" in the endeavor. The leader must allow the teachers to take the lead and play the role of "managing partner," but as a limited partner the principal offers emotional support, material support, and interest in the project. This will require such actions as attending meetings of the team, alerting members to growth opportunities, and being a cheerleader for their efforts. In the first year or two, some principals think it is wise to accept any initiative (created by faculty) that is moving in (roughly) the desired direction of improvement. They see this posture as preferable to being seen as advocating for only the large, significant, or high-risk endeavors. Projecting an accepting image is important because it sets up the leader to accomplish the next part of the process.

Step #2: Providing successful experiences. A key component of a DIP or GLIP is adhering to a timeline, such as the following example:

Development of GLIP	September 15
Sharing of GLIP	September 30
Carrying out GLIP	October-April
Assessment of GLIP	May
Reporting on GLIP	June

Although following a prescribed schedule may at first appear to be overly procedural, having a timeline accomplishes several critical purposes. The development and sharing activity serves as an affirmation. By publicly declaring an intention to pursue an initiative (i.e., writing across the curriculum, implementing thematic instruction, utilizing performance assessment, etc.) the likelihood of follow-through is enhanced. The carrying-out phase is an opportunity for the leader to provide tangible and emotional assistance to each team, thereby helping the members of the group to feel both supported and appreciated.

Assessment and reporting are critical features of the model because it is only through those steps that members can see that their efforts are truly making a difference. Figures 2.4 and 2.5 are examples of DIPs created at a public high school.

Several things are worth noting from these examples. The projects are not of equal significance. The assessment criteria provided utilize a developmental continuum. This means the participants identify possible outcomes ranging from ones they would be delighted with to ones that would be disappointing.

Step #3: Institutionalizing continuous improvement. After the first year and with each subsequent round of DIP or GLIP work, the leader's role of limited partner should become more or less directive as circumstances warrant. When a group has been showing substantial maturity, like the language arts department (whose first effort is illustrated in Figure 2.4), then (during sharing time) the leader would be wise to offer little direction and instead

Target Area

Promote Writing

Activities to Facilitate Reaching the Target Area:

1. Utilize support period to increase coordination across disciplines in the standards for essay writing.
2. Create a schoolwide writing festival.
3. Establish adult writing groups.
4. Offer mini-writing workshops for parents and other community members in order to create awareness of the writing process.
5. Share ideas and strategies for the teaching of writing.
6. Attend workshops and seminars that focus on the writing process.
7. Implement new and varied writing opportunities in the classroom.
8. Cooperate on the production of the literary magazine *Kaleidoscope*.

Resources to Support Activities:

1. Financial support from the school district.
2. Building travel funds for workshops or visits to other districts.
3. Professional Development Fund for conferences.
4. Professional Staff Development Budget.
5. Assistance from the administrators and CCC.

Outcome Expected:

5. After the loss of the Apple Grant, teachers take a stand against sloppy work. Quill and ink become required materials in Penmanship I, II, III, and IV.
4. Writing instruction ends at W.L.H.S. Armed with cans of spray paint, frustrated students deface West Linn city buildings and signs, scrawling, "Trust Measure 2!"

Figure 2.4. Language Arts Department Improvement Plan, 1984-85

> 3. Teachers across the curriculum use the writing process to motivate students, while parents celebrate writing excellence at home.
> 2. Student writers form writing groups. Every Friday, fans, the pep band, cheerleaders, and doting Guardian Angels jam the auditorium to hear readings from the groups.
> 1. The *New York Times* Review of Books opens a branch office in the Old Store to be near brilliant young W.L.H.S. writers.

Figure 2.4. Continued

practice the skill of active listening. If, however, the group has exhibited a significantly lower level of development, then the limited partner (principal) might exercise more influence over the group's work through the strategic use of questioning. In meetings of such less developed work groups the principal might ask:

- What have you been reading lately regarding developmental education, the use of technology, etc?
- What difficulties have students been having in achieving success with your curriculum?
- What would it take to cause every student to be successful with your program?

These types of questions will raise the level of anxiety for faculty, but they do not constitute an authoritarian approach to leadership. Over time, if faculty members are unable or unwilling to respond to such prompts, then a more heavy-handed supervisory response might be called for. But often the gentle prod of a well-chosen question will go a long way toward inspiring introspection.

Once the GLIP or DIP process has been institutionalized in a school the leader can effect substantial transformational change indirectly. What the leader wants to do is, in effect, foster a culture of professional discourse on continuous improvement. Then through immersion in that culture faculty members experience a transformative impact. Figure 2.6 illustrates this transformational leadership process.

> **Department:** Vocational Education
>
> **Target Area** (objective or need):
> Complete and review the assessment of the standards for technology education programs.
>
> **Activities to facilitate reaching the target area:**
> Staff efforts will be directed toward correcting deficiencies noted by the assessment. Staff members not involved in the original assessment will complete the packet.
>
> Resources to support activities:
>
> 1. Group meetings
> 2. Individual attention to programs or updating
> 3. A reassessment in June immediately after school is out
>
> Outcome expected:
>
> 1. Noted deficiencies corrected or in process of correction
> 2. More students enrolled in vocational, technical classes

Figure 2.5. Department Improvement Plan: Vocational Department 1983-84

Encouraging Suppliers to Focus on Quality

Occasionally when one reads the literature on the principalship one concludes that a principal should be the sovereign over his or her own realm. However, anyone who has sat in the principal's chair will attest that the job is anything but free agency. Particularly in the site-based management context the principal is often caught in a particular vise grip that afflicts many modern middle managers. Figure 2.7 illustrates the problem of the site-based pinch.

The problem for the principal in a democratic school is that expectations and demands often come simultaneously from two

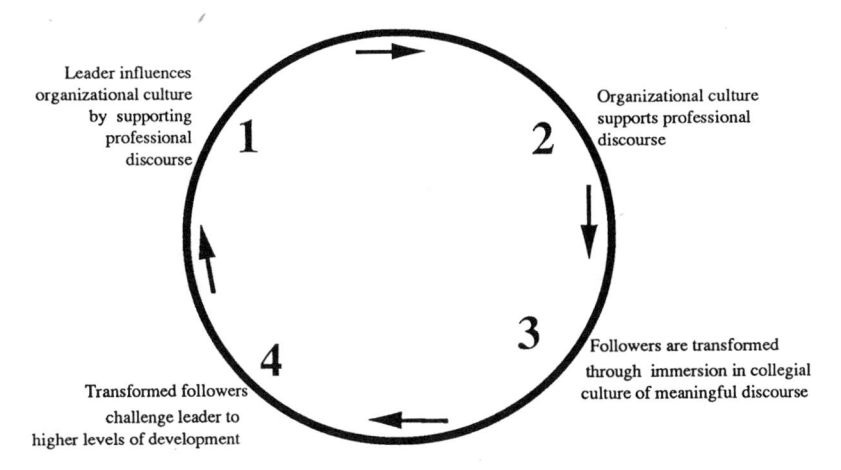

```
        ┌─────────────────┐
Leader influences              Organizational culture
organizational culture          supports professional
by supporting                  discourse
professional    1        2
discourse

              4        3
Transformed followers          Followers are transformed
challenge leader to            through immersion in collegial
higher levels of development   culture of meaningful discourse
```

Figure 2.6. Transformational Leadership Process

directions and the principal is expected to satisfy two masters. This can be difficult, especially if and when these expectations are in conflict. We have identified three strategies that principals can use to help their subordinates focus on quality while managing the site-based pinch.

Strategy #1: Create a Buffer

Educators work inside an open system. Demands for production and performance come from all directions, both inside and outside the organization (Hanson, 1991). That fact accounts for much of the challenges faced by contemporary school leadership, but it can also explain some of the pressure and stress experienced by many of the leaders. For many teachers the locus of external stress is the district. In this case *district* is taken to mean not only the central administration, but also community pressure groups who can make their needs felt through the central administration. The external analysis conducted during the strategic planning process as well as the questions addressed in the vision scope (see chapter 1) are specific ways school leaders can audit

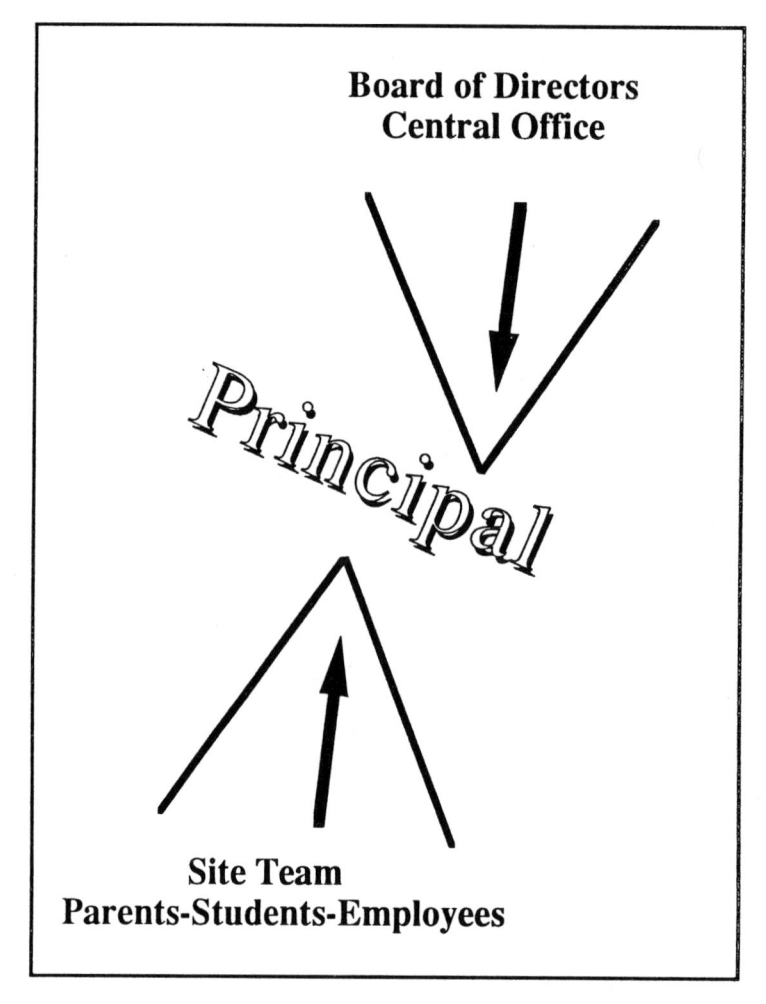

Figure 2.7. The Site-Based Pinch

the pressures being exerted by their different customer groups. Because customers are so varied and their demands often appear contradictory, central administrative responses to outside stimuli often seem to be awfully reactive to the classroom teacher. For example:

- If patrons complain about the sex education curriculum, it instantly comes under review.
- If parents express concern over academic rigor, a review is immediately conducted of homework policies.
- If parents suggest that school is too easy, the superintendent asks teachers to enforce higher expectations.

The cynical teacher often comes to see the central office as a weather vane switching direction with every parental communication. Of course, these teachers may be conditioned by their own context. The central office is responding only to its customers, many of whom are petitioning with emergent problems. The faculty, on the other hand, is more likely to be engaged in carrying out more long-term initiatives that will need lots of time and nurturing to take root. One job of the effective TQE instructional leader is to buffer the teacher/innovators whom they supervise from distracting external demands. As we have often repeated, without a clear vision school leaders will run the risk of demoralizing teachers and alienating parents and the community by being perceived as constantly changing direction and program emphasis.

In a school district that was blessed (or cursed) with an innovative and program-oriented central administration, this phenomenon played itself out in a most interesting way. Three predominant *buffering* styles employed by principals in this district were identified (Sagor, 1992). Buffering by the principal enabled teachers to focus on the task at hand and the content goals for the work group without having their finite energy and organizational focus siphoned off to tangential matters. When dealing with the multiple subcultures and subsystems that existed in the medium-sized school district, principal buffering became the crucial bridge connecting district and building cultures.

Each of the three different buffering styles functioned as a doorway through which the faculty at each school experienced the external environment. Two of the principals functioned like "solid core" wooden doors, two functioned as though they were made of "sculptured glass" (refracting all the light that flowed through them), and two operated as "screen doors" allowing most breezes (external issues) to blow through the leader totally unhindered.

Solid core principals. Sarah was a high school principal. She was a committed, hardworking, and hard-nosed administrator. Although her educational philosophy was in line with that of the superintendent and she had prospered under her superintendent's personal and programmatic support, she sometimes appeared to be in a continuous power struggle with her boss. This notwithstanding, the superintendent consistently received more dedicated support from Sarah than from anyone else in the district. Likewise, Sarah could always be counted on to defend the superintendent against attackers from inside or outside the organization. Nevertheless, Sarah regularly behaved in a manner that caused her to be viewed by faculty as the undisputed "chief executive officer" in her building. To all who worked at the high school, the buck was seen as stopping on Sarah's desk. Generally, she was carrying forth the faculty's agenda, but even when she was going ahead with a district mandate, it was invariably seen as a goal to which she was personally committed. Sarah was just not the type of leader who would ever implore her staff to carry out a project simply "because the superintendent said so!"

The solid core door phenomena appeared also with another, yet very different principal. Janet was a young, vivacious principal serving a small elementary school. Because of the size of her school and her desire to spend more time with her young children, Janet worked on a part-time contract. Although Sarah impressed everyone with her toughness and resolve, one's first impression of Janet conveyed warmth, ease, and softness. However, there was a great deal of determination lying just under the surface. Janet calculated every move very clearly. The superintendent described her interactions with Janet this way:

> Janet is another one who is always gracious, but she can be very stubborn. With things that she feels strongly about, she can be very persistent. And when it comes to something she does feel strongly about—what's right for kids or staff—she makes her case, she makes it strongly, and she doesn't

back off until something's done about it. And I appreciate that about her. She's not a principal who ever calls "wolf." Her issues are legitimate, they're well thought through, and again, when she feels the need to say, "Hey, I need some help here. This is the situation. Now, I expect something in return," she gets it.

Janet didn't petition the central office nearly as much as Sarah did, but when she did it was because she felt she needed to prevail and as the superintendent related, she invariably succeeded. Although these two administrators presented different styles, they both constructed almost impervious buffers between their staff and the district office. By positioning their backs between their building and the district, they allowed their teachers to feel complete ownership of local initiatives. More important, this buffering left the faculty feeling empowered and relatively unencumbered by external pressure.

Sculptured glass principals. Glenn was the master of the sculptured glass door. He was the principal of an elementary school that had experienced several administrators in recent years. All of Glenn's recent predecessors were assertive and had strong curriculum backgrounds, close relationships with the superintendent, and fiery personalities. After 10 years of this type of leader, the teachers found his laid-back style very comforting. Although many faculty appreciated the emotional relief provided by his nondirective style, they also reported appreciating the protection from district pressure that he provided.

Knowing that he needed to be seen by his district as a member of their team and not as a free agent serving only his school, he realized that stonewalling would not be an effective buffering strategy. Rather, he chose to outmaneuver the district office. He accomplished this primarily through careful reconnaissance. Glenn would stay alert to key phrases and other clues about directions that incurred favor at the central office. He would then be sure to incorporate those words into his reports on the improvement efforts at his school. He would also volunteer to be part of any study team or pilot group that was investigating a new initiative.

By using this strategy he guaranteed that his faculty were spared external pressure (because they were viewed as leaders). More important, because they were perceived as ahead of the rest of schools in implementing district policy, they were granted the freedom to tailor new programs as they saw best. Glenn felt comfortable "manipulating" the system because it provided his faculty the freedom they needed to produce a better program for their local customers.

Two junior high schools in this district were studied also. These schools served demographically similar populations; however, they had significantly different professional cultures. At Cougar Junior High School Emmet Smith was principal (formerly the principal at Huskyland Junior High). Emmet was a longtime district staff member. Even to casual observers he seemed to be viewed as an extended family's "good ole Uncle Emmet," not as an innovative educational leader. He was, however, able to translate his interpersonal strengths into an impressive record of program implementation. For example, when the superintendent let it be known that she wanted to see certain middle school concepts introduced into the two junior high schools, Emmet put his school way out in front. Although personally conservative, methodical, and generally slow-moving, he vigorously led this charge, getting teachers out to view model middle schools, arguing successfully for financial support for their planning efforts, and even securing funding for extra daily planning time for his multidisciplinary seventh grade teams. The Cougar Junior High faculty expressed considerable appreciation of the district's support for their work. This positive view of the district role was largely due to Emmet's "manipulating" things to make it appear that his faculty was in the driver's seat.

These two portraits show different operating styles within the sculptured glass approach. Glenn was laid-back and Emmet was fatherly, harried, and nervous, yet both managed to keep their schools ahead of district pressure and, therefore, were free to manage their own destinies.

Screen door principals. Another picture emerged at the other junior high school, Huskyland, and at Chauffeur's Ridge Elementary School. At these schools two relatively inexperienced principals, both new to the district, were struggling to establish themselves. They were both happy to be in the district and knew that their long-term success would be determined by satisfying the superintendent. Buddy at Huskyland and Robin at Chauffeur's Ridge both had adapted to these circumstances by placing only a token screen door between their faculty and the district.

Chauffeur's Ridge was a well-managed school serving a middle-class community. Most district programs operated in the school and were carried out faithfully. For example, the thematic unit that became a part of each elementary school's foray into multidisciplinary teaching involved most of the Chauffeur's Ridge teachers, became a focus for a 2-week instructional unit, and culminated in a well-attended parent night. However, when asked, the faculty said they had no intention of spreading this innovation beyond its mandated 2-week stint because this "district program" required "too much effort."

The Chauffeur's Ridge staff were not without emotion. Their comments about the district reflect some serious concerns:

> We are not considered professional enough to make decisions that directly affect students. We are supposed to be using a building-based management with decisions made by each school, but . . . the superintendent makes the decisions that affect us most with little or no input by the building's staff. This is not building-based management!

When Robin stood aside, avoiding a proactive stance on school improvement issues, she also allowed district expectations to bowl over her staff unimpeded. Not only did this screen door buffer fail to foster realization of the district's focus on thematic instruction, but it fueled faculty cynicism and resentment.

Buddy had the unenviable fortune of following the popular "Uncle Emmet" at Huskyland. Unfortunately, he did not have Emmet's personal power (borne of a long, successful history in the district), self-confidence, or freedom of movement, which could have enabled him to become a stronger buffer between his faculty and the central administration. Many of the Huskyland teachers had a habit of looking on all leadership with suspicion. Thus, many were inclined to fight the middle school concept simply because it had its origins at the district office.

Fundamentally, Huskyland teachers refused to be pushed and viewed this particular "push" coming right through the "screen door" and past their principal. Not only did the screen door provide Buddy with no personal security, it almost ensured faculty resistance to those very change initiatives he was interested in supporting. Huskyland ended up a divided staff as can be seen by these comments about both themselves and their district:

> I am disappointed by the negativity of some individuals (faculty) in regards to students and the district. I generally support the district and don't look for spooks behind every tree or bush.

> I feel it's difficult to keep an optimistic outlook at times. The district has good ideas, wrong approach—they don't have a clue about building-based decisions and push ideas without backing of time and money.

The three buffering styles could be categorized as follows:

Style	Solid Core	Sculptured Glass	Screen Door
Methods	Assertive	Manipulative	Agreeable, to a fault
	"Buck" stops here	"Getting out" in front	"Go along to get along"
Results	Completely buffered	Well buffered	Not buffered at all

It is interesting to note from these examples that based on the principal's buffering style an identical district context was viewed fundamentally differently by different local faculties.

Strategy #2: The Hiring Process

Although Deming shows that personnel are only one piece of the system, the importance of that piece should not be underestimated. Despite the overwhelming attention paid in the education literature about evaluation and supervision, the best way for the school principal to influence the performance of personnel in the school is through a wise and judicious use of the hiring process.

Once a leader has taken the time to foster the shared vision using the strategies outlined in chapter 1, it becomes important to use the staff selection and induction process to reinforce and underscore these shared values. One mechanism for doing this is deliberately focusing on the interview process as having as much to do with teaching the values and beliefs of the organization as it does with the selection of future employees. It is not uncommon in the corporate world to have a recruit spend 1 or 2 days (on-site) as part of the selection/interview process. That time is spent engaged in both formal and informal interviews, observation of the work site, and development of interpersonal relationships. When a candidate leaves such an interview, he or she generally will have a clear understanding of the organizational culture, feel that the organization is vested in getting the best personnel, and have a clear understanding of organizational priorities.

Now let's consider a typical teacher interview:

5 minutes on your background
10 minutes on what you did last summer
15 minutes on your ideas on curriculum
15 minutes listening to the school's philosophy on curriculum
10 minutes for your questions

Is that sufficient devotion of time and energy to get a potential employee off to the right start? Instead, consider this approach to interviewing used by a public high school in Oregon:

8:00	*Arrival.* Candidate arrives, is greeted by the principal, shown to an office by the secretary, given a cup

(Continued)

of coffee, and asked to respond in writing to the following prompt: "Please draft a handout you might be likely to give to your students on the first day of class. Your handout may include any information you deem relevant, but should also include information on: (a) your goals, (b) your grading practices, and (c) your behavioral expectations."

8:45 *Personal interview.* Candidate is interviewed by the assistant principal, who asks a series of questions designed to let the candidate tell who they are, what they value, and what they are looking for professionally. This interview, called "the personal interview," is a chance for the candidates to have the floor to introduce themselves in a manner that is designed to be comfortable.

9:30 *Demonstration teaching.* For the next hour the candidate works in a classroom teaching the school's curriculum. The candidate has had an opportunity to meet with the regular teacher prior to the interview. The department head, the classroom teacher, and several other faculty members observe the lesson.

10:45 *Curriculum and instruction interview.* This is an opportunity for the candidate to debrief the lesson just taught and to walk the interview committee (made up of teachers and administrators) through his or her approach to teaching. The group also discusses the candidate's response to the written prompt that was completed earlier.

12:00 *Lunch with the department.* The candidate is taken to the faculty lunchroom to dine with what may be future colleagues and have their questions answered.

12:45 *Tour of the building.* A vice-principal and the department head take the candidate on a building tour.

1:15 *Good-bye from the principal.* The principal walks the candidate to the door, responds to questions, thanks him or her for coming, and gives a personalized packet of information on the school and its curriculum, program, and goals.

Before gasping at the amount of time invested in each interview by this faculty, consider the importance of the decision they are about to make. If this teacher is hired and stays throughout his or her career, the district will invest well over a million dollars in the teacher. Furthermore, he or she will influence hundreds, perhaps thousands of students. Also, consider that in any given year a high percentage of the faculty will participate in this interview process, further investing them in the quality of the personnel at their school.

Strategy #3: The Induction Process

In the first days and weeks on a job employees are socialized into the norms of their new workplace. The lessons learned in this socialization process become imprinted and may last as long as the employee stays with the organization. As the old phrase goes, "You only have one chance to make a first impression."

Effective instructional leaders utilize deliberate new employee induction programs as a means to manage the socialization process. The high school whose interview process was detailed above followed the hiring decision with a year-long induction program with the following components:

- Day before all teachers report

Each new faculty member has a full day of activities, beginning with a catered continental breakfast and meetings with all support staff who provide assistance (secretaries, librarians, counselors, etc.). This is followed by a luncheon with a senior member from the department (who later serves as a mentor) and a chance for a lengthy (if needed) informal visit with the department head.

- First day of work

New faculty members receive corsages and formal introductions are made to the entire faculty. Each faculty member is given a written, abbreviated vita describing the work and educational history of each of their new colleagues.

- First day of school

At the opening assembly new faculty members are seated in a place of honor and presented to the student body by student leaders.

- First 9 weeks

New faculty are guests for a weekly breakfast with the principal and administrative staff in order to take care of any logistical issues or to provide a forum for raising questions (how to get supplies, additional desks, make a special education referral, etc.). If the new teachers express a desire to have a special resource person join them at these meetings to assist with an issue, the principal makes the arrangements.

- Second 9 weeks

The group of new teachers and the principal custom design a seminar that addresses instructional issues of interest to the group. Items might include grouping of students, questioning strategies, time management, maintaining high expectations, and so forth. The seminar, coordinated by the principal, meets weekly, has graduate credit attached (paid by the school), and features peer observations and coaching.

- Second semester

Teachers are supported in attending classes and staff development activities of their own choosing. They participate in the school's annual "Day in the Life" program in which they shadow students through a seven-period schedule and compare notes on the student school experience.

- End of year

The new teachers are hosted at an off-campus reception by the principal and other administrators where they are encouraged to debrief their first year so that the induction program can be improved for the next cohort of new faculty.

This program was designed to produce several outcomes:

1. To enable the new employee to see that solving faculty logistical problems is the number one priority of the administration
2. To demonstrate that classroom instruction is the number one goal for the school and that the principal is a partner in that process
3. To reflect that collegiality is a valued norm. Over the course of the year each new teacher typically observes a dozen or more colleagues at work in their classrooms
4. To show that continuous learning through professional development is a school norm
5. To make it clear that self-inquiry is supported and valued

By paying attention to both the selection and induction process the leaders in this school made great strides in inculcating the values of continuous improvement into the culture of their faculty.

Key Terms and Concepts

Achievement motivation. An individual is primarily driven to produce evidence of personal accomplishment and success.

Affiliation motivation. An individual is driven to maximize the quality of the interpersonal and professional relationships of those with whom he or she works most closely.

Buffering. Leadership behavior that allows the staff the psychological security to carry out an improvement agenda without interference from political and transitory distractions from both within and outside the organization.

Customer. The individual or group who is in a position to consume the outcomes produced by the enterprise. As the benefi-

48 ✧ The TQE Principal: A Transformed Leader

ciary of the system the customer is in the best position to assess and perceive quality.

Customer-based assessment. Techniques used to solicit and consider the degree of satisfaction that customers hold in the product produced by the system. For example, with schools, customer-based assessment might involve having students, parents, and employers rate the quality of the education received by the students.

DIP/GLIP (Departmental and grade level improvement process/ plan). Structured procedures that help a work group develop the norm of continuous improvement. Leaders wishing to institute DIP/GLIP must concern themselves with readiness, implementation, and institutionalization processes.

Induction. A coherent and thoughtfully carried out process to convey the vision and inculcate the norms of an organization to new employees. It is a process for managing an inevitable socialization process.

Input. The resources available to the system to accomplish its work. For example, inputs in the school system include students, instructional materials, and faculty.

Norm of continuous improvement. The thought processes and patterns of behavior engaged in by groups that are constantly seeking refinements in their processes so that they can produce a better product for their customers.

Output. The product produced by a system as a result of carrying out its work. In the case of schools, outputs include the knowledge, skills, and character attributes that are possessed by graduates.

Power motivation. An individual is driven to play a role where he or she can exercise maximum control over his or her own work environment and the work of others.

Priority pie. A technique to graphically display the elements of a system and the weight they hold in determining systemic effectiveness. Priority pies can be used by leaders to align their time and effort with the factors that matter the most in terms of organizational effectiveness.

Systemic thinking. The perspective taken by a leader that takes into account inputs and throughputs as well as outcomes. Systemic thinkers view personnel as only one part of a complex process.

Throughput. The processes used by the system when carrying out its work. For example, throughputs in the school system include curriculum, instructional activities, teaching, and testing.

References

Berman, P., & McLaughlin, M. (1974). *Federal programs supporting educational change.* Santa Monica, CA: Rand Corporation.

Corbett, H. D., Dawson, J., & Firestone, W. (1984). *School context and school change.* New York: Teachers College Press.

Deming, W. E. (1986). *Out of crisis.* Cambridge: MIT Center for Advanced Engineering Study.

Edmonds, R. (1979). Effective schools for the urban poor. *Educational Leadership, 37,* 15-24.

Fullan, M., & Stiegelbauer, S. (1991). *The new meaning of educational change.* New York: Teachers College Press.

Hall, G. E., & Hord, S. (1987). *Change in schools: Facilitating the process.* Albany: SUNY Press.

Hanson, M. E. (1991). *Educational administration and organizational behavior.* Boston: Allyn & Bacon.

Sagor, R. (1992). *Growing effective schools: The influence of district context.* Paper presented at AERA annual meeting, San Francisco.

Senge, P. M. (1990). *The fifth discipline: The art and practice of the learning organization.* New York: Doubleday Currency.

Sergiovanni, T. J., & Starratt, R. J. (1993). *Supervision: A redefinition.* New York: McGraw-Hill.

✧ 3 ✧

Optimizing the Talents of All Staff Members

Teachers in most school organizations spend about one third of their adult working lives engaged in tasks associated with their jobs. If their daily work routines become dull and uninspiring, teachers can lose their enthusiasm for teaching, learning, and professional growth. Besides being paid salaries that often are not commensurate with their skills and training, the education profession is constantly pressured to increase student achievement, improve the quality of teaching, and solve the social ills plaguing society. These factors pose a severe challenge for instructional leaders who wish to create schools that are exciting and vibrant places for teachers and students. Although instructional leaders can help to promote teachers' interest and commitment by enlisting the ideas expressed in chapter 1 about visioning, they also need to understand how adults learn and develop in order to unleash the talents of teachers and promote their professional growth.

One of the important features of TQE is that all individuals in the organization must feel joy in their work, their talents must be utilized, and they must be constantly encouraged to improve. Therefore, this chapter will focus on three areas that instructional leaders need to be aware of and attend to in order to ensure a work climate that nurtures growth, professional respect, and mutual support:

1. Leaders must understand the principles of adult learning and model continuous learning.
2. Leaders must be able to read the current culture of their school settings and to establish traditions and rituals that acknowledge exemplary performance and improvement.
3. Leaders must optimize the talents of the teaching staff by trusting their expertise and encouraging and supporting teachers in their efforts to become leaders.

How Adults Learn

As we discussed in chapter 2, the adults' emotional needs for power, achievement, and affiliation can be strong motivators of work performance. In working with teachers, principals also need to be aware of the ways in which adults learn best. In most school settings, the range of ages and background experiences of a teaching staff can be quite extensive. For example, it would not be uncommon for a school staff to include teachers who have taught nearly 30 years and are nearing retirement to novice teachers who may be in their early 20s and have only 1 or 2 years of teaching experience. This says nothing of differences in family background, gender, race, and parental experience. In short, a school staff can be a diverse makeup of teachers who have different attitudes about students and teaching, career aspirations, and personal likes and dislikes.

Principles of Adult Learning

Given this array of experiences and motivations, principals must develop a keen awareness of how adults learn and develop if they are to create an environment in which everyone feels like a contributing, successful member of the organization. The growing literature base on adult learning provides guidance for principals in their attempts to facilitate teachers' growth (Merriam & Caffarella, 1991). In particular, six components of adult learning need to be understood and responded to:

- The rich experiential background of adults
- Their need for affiliation
- Their desire for active involvement
- The learning processes of adults
- The influence of significant life events on learning
- The importance of lifelong learning

Rich experiential background. A distinct difference between adults and children is the quantity and quality of social and professional experiences adults have accumulated. This rich reservoir of experiences serves as a source of self-identity for many adults. Their experiences, therefore, become an important learning resource for individuals as well as for groups of adults. Often as adults reexamine their experiences, they tend to reintegrate or modify the meaning of these events in light of a current situation. Instructional leaders can facilitate teachers' learning by allowing them to discuss and process their life experiences, especially as new reform efforts, such as shared decision making and integrated curriculum, are being introduced in schools.

Affiliation needs. Rather than being motivated by power or achievement, many adults want to receive and to provide support to other adults (see chapter 2). Human contact, understanding, and mutual involvement in decision making are important aspects of adults' experiences. By forming personal and professional relationships, adults are better able to process their learning experiences and to create effective work groups. The suggestions for developing a collegial work environment advocated later in this chapter are good examples of how instructional leaders can capitalize on adults' shared need to engage in meaningful and productive relationships.

Active involvement. Instead of being passive recipients of information, most adults prefer to be actively involved in the learning process. They appreciate opportunities to actively process information and engage in hands-on activities. If instructional leaders share information using only a lecture-style approach, they run the risk of teachers not remembering the information or being less than enthusiastic about applying the information.

Learning processes. Three important factors regarding the learning processes of adults need to be considered in their growth and development: meaningfulness, pacing, and transfer. Allowing adults to determine the meaning or usefulness of new information is particularly important because if they do not see the relevance of a particular activity or event, they are likely to be involved at only a superficial level. Pacing refers to the time involved in examining a problem, processing it, and responding. Studies indicate that as adults grow older, the time required to engage in these processes increases. Finally, adults may have difficulty transferring knowledge from one situation to another or learning new material. For example, whereas some adults may be particularly adept at designing learning activities for most children, they may not be able to transfer this knowledge when working with special needs students (e.g., disabled or special education students). Perceptive instructional leaders get to know the individual capabilities of the teaching staff, which allows them to be supportive rather than judgmental (see chapter 4).

Significant life events. The lives of adults are becoming increasingly complex. The typical teacher, for example, takes on a host of other roles such as friend, mother/father, sister/brother, daughter/son, community member, neighbor, and consumer. On occasion, these other roles conflict with being a teacher. Tragic family events or financial concerns can inhibit a teacher's ability to concentrate on the job. By being aware of the personal situations of the teaching staff, instructional leaders can be sensitive to particular instances when teachers may need additional understanding and support.

Modeling continuous learning. Besides understanding how other adults learn and encouraging their growth and development, instructional leaders need to be aware of how they themselves can model lifelong learning. The mission statements illustrated in chapter 1 all indicate the importance of lifelong learning for students;

the same should hold also for instructional leaders. Roland Barth, for example, echoes this thought as he contends that one measure of success for principals is to become the "head learner." Unfortunately, a myth exists in education that principals need to have all the answers at their fingertips and the knowledge and expertise to handle any situation that arises. Such an image of the all-knowing and omnipotent instructional leader is misleading because this suggests the leader is a stagnant learner who already knows everything there is to know with no room for self-improvement, self-understanding, or new knowledge. Although teachers do want an instructional leader who is competent and knowledgeable (see chapter 4), they also appreciate a leader who acknowledges mistakes, recognizes opportunities for personal growth, and models the importance of continuous learning by participating in professional development activities.

One way principals can model their commitment to continuous learning is to directly communicate what they are learning to the teaching staff. As they attend workshops, seminars, or university courses, principals can share new ideas with the staff. A particularly powerful way to demonstrate their resolve to learn new skills is to engage in a peer shadowing or coaching process with other principals. For example, the Peer-Assisted Leadership program developed by the staff at the Far West Regional Laboratory encourages principals to observe one another as they go about their daily activities, providing feedback afterward in the form of a reflective interview (Barnett, 1987). Principals who have participated in this peer observation program mention that their credibility with teachers increases because they are willing to risk being observed by another professional just as teachers are forced to do when observed by principals.

To analyze the degree to which continuous learning is recognized and modeled, instructional leaders can ask themselves the questions in the self-inventory described in Figure 3.1. Based on the answers, leaders can identify areas of strength and improvement as a continuous learner. To discover the perceptions of the teaching staff, this inventory can be reworded and completed anonymously by teachers. A comparison of the perceptions of the

	Never	Sometimes	Often	Always
1. I admit mistakes to teachers.	1	2	3	4
2. I admit mistakes to parents.	1	2	3	4
3. I admit mistakes to my superiors.	1	2	3	4
4. If there is a disagreement, my solution usually is the most appropriate.	1	2	3	4
5. I am a self-directed learner.	1	2	3	4
6. If I don't know something, I try to find out about it only if someone tells me to.	1	2	3	4
7. If I don't know an answer, I am reluctant to let other people know.	1	2	3	4
8. I'm willing to try a new idea even if the risk of failure is high.	1	2	3	4
9. I participate in professional development activities on a regular basis.	1	2	3	4
10. I share new knowledge from my professional development activities with teachers.	1	2	3	4

Figure 3.1. Inventory of the Principal's Continuous Learning and Improvement

leaders with the teachers' reactions can reveal potential areas for growth and improvement.

Dealing With School Culture

Because proponents of TQM, especially Deming, take a systems perspective, leaders must understand how the norms of the school organization influence outcomes. Furthermore, a guiding principle of TQM is that leaders must strive to "... provide for a culture of shared values. This includes how employees work together in an environment of fairness, openness, trust, clear standards, and respect for the dignity of others" (Downey, 1992, p. 208). Therefore, besides knowing how adults learn, principals need to be aware of how the school culture contributes to or detracts from teachers' enjoyment, sense of purpose, and motivation. The concept of culture was first introduced by anthropologists to explain the dynamics of group interaction in tribal and societal communities. Recently, this concept has been incorporated as a means for understanding the patterns of behavior that affect an organization's goals. Although there are numerous definitions of culture, this concept is based on the assumption that organizations have a "way of doing business" that encompasses a set of shared beliefs, values, and acceptable behaviors that help members of the organization function effectively, ultimately shaping how they view the organization and its work.

Clearly, engaging in a strategic planning or visioning process (see chapter 1) is a means for discovering, assessing, and/or altering the manner in which people in an organization choose to believe and behave. There are, however, a variety of more subtle activities principals can engage in to determine what people believe and value. Deal and Peterson (1990) suggest the following ways for principals to "read" the current school culture:

1. Reconstruct the history of the school by developing an organizational genealogy or family tree of the school. This can be done informally by listening to and watching other people and by examining artifacts, such as yearbooks, news-

paper clippings, and previous program or school evaluations. Another strategy might be to conduct a formal inservice session where the history of the school can be recreated through stories told by the long-term faculty who can recall important events, people, and activities.
2. Listen to people as they talk about the school and how it operates. These people can take on different cultural roles such as priests and priestesses, storytellers, gossips, spies, counterspies, and moles.
3. Ask questions about past events, current events, and future aspirations. These questions might include: What important events occurred in the school's history, how were they resolved, and who was involved? What do people say about the school's present stature? What do people hope or dream about for the school?

Beyond reading the current culture, principals can shape the culture to be compatible with the vision or direction in which the school is headed. In particular, they can establish ceremonies, traditions, and rituals that celebrate the achievements and talents of the teaching staff. Recognition dinners, certificates of achievement, written notes of appreciation, and constant verbal reminders to the teaching staff about their importance and value to the school are routines that shape the culture. By recognizing the important role staff members play in the lives of students and the community, principals can make the school a more joyful and rewarding place to work. To determine whether traditions and rituals need to be created, principals can answer the questions on the following checklist.

Checklist for Determining How the Culture Recognizes and Values Teachers

- What does the local media print about schools and individual teachers?
- How are teachers greeted formally and informally on returning to school each fall?

- How does the school year end?
- What ceremonies, traditions, or rituals currently exist to recognize teachers' individual and collective efforts?
- What do students and parents say about the teaching staff?
- What do students and parents do formally and informally to acknowledge teachers' efforts?
- What professional development opportunities are provided to teachers? Do they appreciate these opportunities or find them useless?
- On a daily basis, what do you do to show your appreciation for teachers?
- How do teachers treat one another? Do they value one another's contributions to the school?
- Are there some teachers who are viewed as being excellent or deficient by their peers? By their students? By parents? By you?

Based on the results of this checklist, principals can approach teachers for their ideas about how best to develop activities and events that acknowledge teachers' contributions. For instance, if the survey indicates teachers feel underappreciated and have little time to engage in professional dialogue, principals might learn from talking to teachers that they would like to devote time during faculty meetings to acknowledge different teachers' accomplishments, to begin a "teacher of the week" campaign, or to initiate a peer coaching program (see chapter 4). As these new activities are put in place, principals can listen to teachers' comments and observe their interactions to determine if these measures are having the desired effect on the school culture.

Recognizing the Talents of Teacher Leaders

Beyond creating a culture that merely celebrates the talents and accomplishments of teachers, instructional leaders sensitive to the principles of TQE need to show that they value the judgments and expertise of the teaching faculty. Putting notes in teachers' mailboxes, telling them they are doing a good job, sponsoring a year-end banquet to recognize their achievements, or having the local media publish occasional articles about teachers does much to recognize their efforts, but does not overtly demonstrate trust in their expertise. To show teachers they are trusted professionals means giving them ample opportunity to share their knowledge and expertise and to make decisions. Therefore, instructional leaders can demonstrate this high level of trust by allowing teachers to build a collegial work environment through sharing their time and talents with one another and by developing the capacity of teachers to become instructional leaders.

Creating Collegial Work Environments

The structure of most schools is such that teachers rarely have the chance to work collaboratively on aspects related to teaching. Clearly, in this era of shared decision making, teachers have more involvement in the direction of the policies and practices associated with instructional programs, budgets, student assessment strategies, and hiring new staff; however, they often are not able to focus on their true area of expertise—teaching. Because most teachers work in isolated classrooms or departments (a point we will expand on later in chapter 5), they rarely observe one another's teaching or work together on teaching projects (except in the instances of team teaching used in many middle schools). As such, teachers are not able to share their craft knowledge about teaching on a regular basis.

What then can instructional leaders do to allow the expertise of teachers to be shared? Judith Warren Little (1982), for instance, has discovered schools can foster a collegial learning environment when the school culture encourages and supports continuous discussions about teaching, experimentation, and risk taking. To demonstrate trust in teachers' abilities while creating the conditions for experimentation and collegiality to thrive, instructional leaders can:

- Encourage teachers to observe one another and provide feedback about their teaching. Peer coaching (described more fully in chapter 4) can be supported.
- Allow groups of teachers to visit other schools to see first-hand how others are dealing with common areas of concern. On their return, teachers can meet with their peers to share their insights.
- Support teachers' efforts to jointly prepare and deliver instructional materials.
- Provide opportunities for teachers to engage in demonstration lessons for one another. Besides having teachers conduct lengthy in-service sessions for one another, faculty or department meetings can be held in different teachers' classrooms and the host teacher(s) can briefly demonstrate a teaching activity he or she is currently using.
- Encourage teachers to participate in collaborative action research projects with their peers and outside consultants (e.g., district personnel, university faculty). The benefits and factors contributing to successful collaborative action research will be discussed later in examining the professionalization of teaching (see chapter 5).

Involving teachers in these types of interactions builds directly on the adult learning principles presented earlier in this chapter. For instance, teachers' extensive knowledge and experience bases are tapped, their need to affiliate with other adults is acknowledged, and they are encouraged to be actively involved in learning with and from their teaching colleagues.

A clear challenge for principals who desire this level of collegial interaction among teachers requires them to locate the resources needed to allow these activities to occur during school time rather than only before or after school. This means principals and teachers need to schedule classroom assignments such that teachers have blocks of time to plan activities and/or to hire substitutes to cover classroom assignments while teachers work together or visit other school sites. There also is no reason why principals cannot occasionally take over teachers' classrooms to allow them to have the time to work with their teaching peers on collaborative projects.

Developing Teacher Leaders

Besides working jointly to design and deliver classroom curricular materials and activities, teachers also can take on formal and informal leadership roles in dealing with instructional issues and schoolwide concerns (e.g., school-community relations, scheduling). Formally, teachers can participate in leadership teams, such as school improvement committees, accountability committees, collaborative decision-making committees, leadership management teams, and school advisory councils. In some cases, these teams address issues identified by the school principal; in other instances, teams deal with emerging issues such as parental involvement, fund-raising, and discipline policies.

An important feature of these types of teams is whether they advise the principal or have the ultimate authority to make decisions or policies that must be abided by. Of the leadership teams investigated by Blase and Kirby (1992), over half (60%) acted in an advisory capacity to the principal. It is helpful for team members to know beforehand the formal authority they have or the manner in which their decisions will be viewed. Some school districts and schools provide guidance to teams regarding their ultimate responsibility in the decision-making process. For instance, teams can engage in three types of decisions: *shared decisions, input decisions,* and *administrative decisions.* Shared decisions include issues the teaching staff has ultimate responsibility for overseeing and implementing. Input decisions are made by the principal with assistance or guidance from team members. Administrative decisions are actions taken by the principal without any formal input from teachers; these decisions must adhere to the school board's policy and master contract. The chart below provides examples of the kinds of issues falling within each of these three decision-making areas.

Shared decisions. Made by teachers who implement the decisions and are held accountable for their results:

Mission and belief statements
Student grouping assignments
Student conduct code
Staff development plans
School improvement goals

Input decisions. Made by the principal with teacher input and guidance:
Room assignments
Student classroom assignments
Budget allocations
Master schedules
Hiring new staff
Field trips
Agendas for staff meetings

Administrative decisions. Made by principal without teacher input:
Teacher evaluations and dismissals
Classified staff evaluations and dismissals
Leave requests for teachers
Fire/tornado drills
Student suspensions and expulsions

These formal leadership responsibilities need not always occur collectively as teachers participate in leadership teams, committees, or task forces. For instance, individual teachers may be selected to work as lead teachers with their peers. In one school district, for example, each year the teaching staff in a school identifies and selects a teacher who serves in the capacity as a teacher leader, working closely with teachers in developing materials, teaching lessons, and evaluating student performance. Not only does this person have the respect and admiration of his or her peers as an outstanding teacher, but he or she also is given a half-time release from the teaching assignment to work with teachers during the school day.

In beginning to better understand what is meant by a *teacher leader*, Fay (1991) provides the following definition: "A teacher leader is a practicing teacher who is chosen by the faculty to lead it in ways determined by the context of school needs and who has formal preparation and scheduled time for leadership that, to preserve the teacher mission, calls for neither managerial nor supervisory duties" (p. 158).

Because there is not a precedent for identifying and supporting teacher leaders in most schools, instructional leaders need to be keenly aware of how this role affects teacher leaders, other teachers, students, and administrators. Several recent investigations of teacher leaders reveal their perceptions about taking on this new role, noting the excitement and difficulties that arise (e.g., Fay, 1991; Wilson, 1993). These preliminary studies provide the following portrait of teacher leaders:

- They constantly are searching for ways to grow personally and professionally.
- They want to maintain the distinction between being a teacher leader and being an administrator.
- They are concerned about maintaining their collegial relationships with other teachers.
- They do not always see themselves as leaders based on their teaching role.
- They believe the school day needs to be restructured and teacher time must be used differently.
- They have clear ideas about classroom goals, but not about a schoolwide shared vision.
- They desire training and professional development to support this new role.

Personal and professional growth. Teachers leaders are not content with their current knowledge and expertise. Their attitude is that they still have much to learn about and actively seek new challenges that will promote their own growth as well as the development of their students. As one teacher leader stated: "Today was something different. We worked on a grant-writing project and are submitting a building grant proposal. We are so excited about it that we can hardly see straight" (Wilson, 1993, p. 24).

The astute principal needs to capitalize on the thirst for new knowledge and experiences these teacher leaders crave. These teachers should be acknowledged for their efforts and should be allowed to share their knowledge, skills, and enthusiasm with other teachers. The hope is that their attitudes would become infectious, creating a collegial school culture where the norm is to publicly share their positive teaching experiences, joys, and accomplishments.

Distinction between teacher leadership and administration. Teacher leaders do not want to be perceived as being other administrators who supervise teachers and manage the school's operations. They want their power and authority to come from their peers based on the respect the teaching staff has for their knowledge and skills rather than on their formal positions. Teacher leaders want to support, nurture, and collaborate with their teaching peers about important instructional matters. In some cases, principals find this notion of "earned power" to be uncomfortable, especially if they are not comfortable dealing with teacher input in decision making or if they prefer authority to be given to people based on an established chain of command (e.g., department chair). Enlightened principals, therefore, need to refrain from putting teacher leaders in the position of evaluating their peers, providing information that may be of a confidential nature between a teacher and the teacher leader, making budgetary decisions, or determining teachers' work assignments.

Collegial relationships. Refraining from supervisory and managerial tasks is one way for teacher leaders to maintain their collegial relationship with other teachers. To be effective in this leadership role, however, they also need to be viewed as credible and knowledgeable resources to teachers, to be sensitive to their colleagues' viewpoints, and to acknowledge the expertise and experience of their fellow teachers. How teacher leaders are selected can greatly influence the collegial relationship between teacher leaders and the teachers with whom they work. If principals make autocratic, administrative decisions without the involvement of other teachers when selecting teacher leaders, they run the risk of sabotaging the process. One solution is to put the selection process entirely in the hands of teachers, allowing them to make a shared decision.

Interaction between teacher and leadership roles. In most cases, teacher leaders continue to teach while taking on a leadership role with their peers. In fact, their expertise as teachers is what distinguishes them as leaders in the eyes of many of their peers. Therefore, while teacher leaders appear to be in a position to model collaborative decision making for the teaching staff, many teacher leaders do not perceive themselves as being role models for their colleagues because of their superior teaching abilities. Principals must not only acknowledge the role these leaders can play in improving the quality of instruction and in affecting students outside their own classroom, but also provide resources to support teacher leaders. Principals can engage in the following behind-the-scenes actions to assist teacher leaders in their efforts to work with novice and experienced teachers:

- Provide new teachers with an orientation to the district's and the school's policies and procedures.
- Share current and upcoming district initiatives with the teaching staff.
- Obtain the necessary resources (e.g., textbooks, supplies) teachers need to ensure a quality learning environment for students.
- Locate the funds needed for teachers to attend workshops, visit other schools, and/or develop instructional materials.
- Minimize the amount of paperwork teachers must submit.
- Refrain from interrupting teachers during their classroom instruction.
- Keep scheduled staff and departmental meetings to a minimum.

Restructuring school day and teacher time. Without the time to work with teachers during the school day, teacher leaders will be hampered in their ability to assist teachers in a meaningful way. Peer coaching, for instance, is viewed by teacher leaders as a powerful learning opportunity for teachers willing to engage in mutual observation and feedback. Not only must teacher leaders be given release time, but the remaining teachers must be allowed to meet individually and collectively with teacher leaders and their peers during the school day. To expect teachers to always devote their personal time before or after school fails to recognize their needs as adult learners. Principals can release teachers for periods of time by restructuring the school schedule to allow for common planning time, finding funds to hire substitutes and to conduct staff retreats, and covering classes for teachers.

Classroom goals versus schoolwide vision. Teacher leaders see themselves first and foremost as teachers. As such, they do not always feel capable or are unwilling to provide direction for the entire school community. This visionary, schoolwide leadership role, they believe, falls on the shoulders of other leaders such as principals and superintendents. If, as we advocated in chapter 1, everyone in the school needs to see how his or her work contributes to the school's vision, then teacher leaders can be instrumental in helping other teachers to integrate their goals with the overall direction of the school. The implication for principals is that they may need to initially spend time working with teacher leaders in the visioning process or in developing vision statements or educational platforms to have them see how their individual beliefs, goals, and aspirations fit with the overall aims of the organization. Once these teacher leaders become more comfortable with their sense of efficacy in building and supporting a schoolwide vision, they can begin to work collaboratively with other teachers to help them through this same process.

Training and professional development. Most teacher leaders do not have any formal preparation for this new role. Often the assumption is that because a teacher works well with students, he or she will automatically be able to work effectively with adults. Due to the unique nature of adults as learners discussed earlier in this chapter, teacher leaders need assistance in dealing effectively with their teaching peers. Just as principals need to provide resources for the teaching staff to engage in professional development activities, they also must be sensitive to the needs of teacher leaders. Some of the types of skills teacher leaders need to develop include observation and feedback strategies, group processing, consensus building, conflict resolution, alternative student assessment practices, and communication with different school publics (e.g., parents, community leaders, school board members).

To create a school culture in which teachers feel they are contributing members of the organization, in which self-improvement is the norm, and in which teacher leadership flourishes, principals must be optimistic. They must constantly look for the good and positive in people, rather than trying to find their weaknesses. The adage "Expect the best and that is what you get; expect the worst, and your expectations will be realized" could never be more appropriate. Teachers want and need to be appreciated for their efforts; they also desire opportunities to affiliate with other adults, rather than working with only students throughout the school day. The transformed instructional leader, therefore, creates a caring culture where teachers are trusted as instructional experts.

Before we go on, it is important to place this emphasis on teacher development in context. Although it is true that the students (not the teachers) are the primary customers of the school, it is also true that the effective functioning of the system is critical to achieving customer satisfaction. Education is a labor-intensive enterprise. The work and attitude of the professional staff is a critical systemic aspect of educational process. Therefore, attending to the staff's development needs is the educational equivalent of a manufacturer securing and maintaining state of the art equipment. For the instructional leader, a focus on the staff development is an investment in throughputs. Chapter 4 examines in greater depth the theme of principals coaching teachers, rather than judging them

Key Terms and Concepts

Administrative decisions. Decisions typically made by the principal without input from other people. Usually these actions are dictated by school district policy and/or the master contract.

Characteristics of adult learners. The factors to consider when working with adults, including their vast number of experiences, their need to interact with other adults, their desire to be actively involved in learning, the way they process information, and how significant life events can affect their learning.

Collegiality. The professional interactions that occur between educators. For teachers, collegiality has been described as their ability to talk precisely about teaching and learning based on observing one another, visiting other schools, jointly developing and delivering instructional materials, conducting demonstration lessons, and participating in collaborative action research projects.

Continuous learning. The recognition by professionals that they still have a need to possess new knowledge and skills as well as the willingness to engage in formal and informal learning experiences to obtain these new understandings and competences.

Input decisions. Decisions ultimately made by the principal based on ideas generated by teachers.

School culture. The set of shared norms, beliefs, values, and acceptable behaviors that exist in a school.

Shared decisions. Decisions made jointly by teachers and administrators where teachers are responsible for implementing the decision and are held accountable for the consequences of the decision.

Teacher leaders. Teachers who are recognized by their peers as outstanding teachers and based on this earned respect have the opportunity to assist in the growth and development of other teachers. These teachers, however, do not want the formal authority to evaluate their teaching colleagues.

References

Barnett, B. G. (1987). Peer-assisted leadership: Using peer observations and feedback as catalysts for professional growth. In J.

Murphy & P. Hallinger (Eds.), *Approaches to administrative training in education* (pp. 131-149). New York: SUNY Press.

Blase, J., & Kirby, P. C. (1992). *Bringing out the best in teachers: What effective principals do.* Newbury Park, CA: Corwin.

Deal, T. E., & Peterson, K. D. (1990). *The principal's role in shaping school culture.* Washington, DC: Office of Educational Research and Improvement.

Downey, C. J. (1992). Applying the quality fit framework to the curriculum management audit. *Education, 113,* 203-209.

Fay, C. F. (1991). *Teacher empowerment through teacher leadership: A new paradigm.* Unpublished doctoral dissertation. Bloomington: Indiana University.

Little, J. W. (1982). Norms of collegiality and experimentation: Workplace conditions of school success. *American Educational Research Journal, 19,* 325-340.

Merriam, S. B., & Caffarella, R. S. (1991). *Learning in adulthood.* San Francisco: Jossey-Bass.

Wilson, M. (1993). The search for teacher leaders. *Educational Leadership, 50,* 24-27.

✧ 4 ✧

Being Coaches and Counselors—
Not Judges

Principals, because of their positions in the school organization, often are forced to make judgments that directly affect the teaching staff. On one hand, principals are required to oversee the school's operation and to formally supervise and evaluate teachers. These supervisory responsibilities obligate them to make decisions about whether teachers are retained, released, or put on probationary status. In short, principals are sometimes forced to judge the competence of teachers. As we discussed in chapter 3 about teacher leadership, this supervisory or managerial function is precisely what teachers want to avoid when taking on a teacher leadership role. On the other hand, many teachers believe principals should make judgments based on their position and status in the organization. Everyone has heard teachers claim, "Well, she's being paid to make the tough decisions, so she shouldn't be asking us to do her dirty work." The prevailing sentiment in many schools is that teachers are paid to teach and principals are paid to administer.

These conditions and attitudes result in situations that often pit principals against teachers. Some educators have argued that because of the evaluatory nature of their jobs, there will always be an adversarial relationship between teachers and principals such that teachers will never be able to fully trust the intentions and actions of principals. These circumstances create quite a dilemma for principals, especially the transformed principal who wants to be an instructional leader by building a collegial and collaborative culture in which teachers and administrators can move to new levels of mutual regard and performance. Even the best of their intentions may be met with suspicion and mistrust. Many novice principals, for example, are surprised at how their seemingly innocent remarks are viewed as being critical or judgmental by teachers. As principals gain experience in their new roles, they become more sensitive about their choice of words—when to be humorous and when to speak publicly or privately with teachers.

What then, is a principal to do? According to the TQE philosophy, leaders lead best by coaching and counseling other people rather than judging, cajoling, or pressuring them. They also must be perceived to be an honest and credible resource to teachers. As their credibility grows, principals are in a much better position to coach or counsel teachers. This chapter examines the specific ways in which principals can build their credibility by coaching and counseling teachers. In particular, the chapter focuses on: (a) how principals can employ direct and nondirect actions to support teachers and to gain credibility as an instructional resource for teachers and (b) how principals can model the elements of coaching and encourage teachers to engage in the peer coaching process.

Providing Support to Teachers

The most common complaints of teachers about a principal's role in supervising or evaluating their instructional approaches are captured in these all too frequently heard comments:

> The principal has visited my classroom only once the whole year. And he only stayed for 5 minutes. How can he even pretend to understand what my goals are or what I'm trying to get the kids to learn?

> When was the last time she was a classroom teacher? The only thing she knows about teaching is what she did 15 years ago. Times and students have changed.

> After he observed my class, he couldn't even give me one piece of advice. I don't think he would know good teaching if it bit him on the nose.

For most classroom teachers, the only way for educators to maintain their credibility about teaching is to continue to teach. The everyday demands of planning lessons, preparing materials, engaging students in stimulating and educational activities, assessing what students are learning, and communicating with parents define what teachers are about. Once a person stops doing these tasks to become an administrator, he or she loses touch with the day-to-day realities of the job. In other countries, such as Canada and England, school administrators are known as head teachers, who teach part of the day and perform administrative duties the remainder of the day. Except in some rural school districts in the United States, the opportunity to continue teaching while being a principal is quite rare. On becoming a principal, educators usually lose the daily contact with students that they enjoyed as teachers.

Although principals may not be responsible for instructing groups of students, there are different actions they can engage in to support the instructional efforts of teachers while at the same time building their own credibility as a viable resource for teachers. In destroying the myth that true instructional leaders spend most of their time teaching classes and/or observing teachers, researchers such as Richard Andrews (Smith & Andrews, 1989) and Ching-Jen Liu (1984) have discovered the direct and indirect ways in which principals can support and guide the instructional process.

Direct Supportive Behaviors

Principals can support teachers' efforts by directly working with them on instructional matters. This requires principals to possess a working knowledge of different instructional techniques, an ability to clearly articulate this knowledge, and a capacity to help teachers link their personal classroom goals with the school's vision. In particular, there are four types of direct actions principals can engage in with teachers:

Conduct frequent classroom observations. Providing direct input to teachers about how their classrooms are organized, how instruction is delivered, and how student performance is assessed are important ingredients in facilitating teachers' professional growth. This requires principals to frequently observe teachers' classroom performances, to provide meaningful feedback during postconferences, to share recent research findings on effective instructional and assessment techniques, to work collaboratively with teachers in interpreting test results, and to communicate how district goals relate to teachers' goals and the school's vision.

Encourage participation in staff development. Often, principals must use outside resources to facilitate the growth and development of teachers. Not only do they need to be knowledgeable about available professional development resources, but also they must be willing to provide ongoing support and release time for teachers to attend staff development sessions, to meet with other teachers to discuss the implications of their new knowledge for the particular school context, to observe one another as they begin implementing new practices, and to critique how well these new practices are addressing the needs of students and the school community. Principals must also be aware of the variety of approaches to staff development in order to meet the different learning needs of their staff (Sparks & Loucks-Horsley, 1989). The most common staff development strategies include:

- Individually guided staff development: Teachers develop personal goals and establish a learning plan to accomplish these goals.
- Observation/assessment: Classroom observations are conducted to provide objective data and feedback to teachers.
- Involvement in a development/improvement process: Teachers work together to create new curriculum and school programs.
- Inquiry: After selecting an area for improvement, teachers collect data, analyze it, and make appropriate adjustments.
- Training: Through participation in individual or group instructional sessions, teachers gain new knowledge and skills.

Constantly communicate about instruction. In chapter 3 we described how a collegial learning environment was one in which discussions of teaching and learning characterize the interactions between teachers and administrators. This does not happen by accident, but must be modeled and nurtured by the principal. Besides being sensitive to teachers' desires and understanding their needs as adult learners, principals must be able to write and speak effectively, actively engage teachers in conflict resolution and problem solving, use a variety of group processing skills, and allow teachers to communicate their instructional needs and expertise with one another. This last point, communication between teachers, can be strongly supported through peer coaching, which will be examined later in this chapter.

Be visible. Rather than sitting in the office doing paperwork or making phone calls, the principal can support instructional activities by being a visible presence throughout the school building. Not only does this include dropping into classrooms, but also meeting school buses when students arrive at school or leave at the end of the day; wandering the hallways, grounds, and cafeteria to monitor student traffic patterns and discussions as well as the physical condition of the school; visiting the teachers' lounge to learn of teachers' concerns and plans; and attending departmental or grade level meetings to hear about ongoing events and activities (Frase, 1992). By increasing their visibility throughout the school building, principals get a sense of the "heartbeat" of the school and can learn about potential concerns before they become major problems. This also is a way to read the current culture of the school. Being physically present also communicates to other people that what they are doing is important enough for the principal to spend time being involved.

Indirect Supportive Behaviors

Besides working directly with teachers to support their instructional efforts, principals can do things to create the conditions that facilitate teachers' abilities to teach. These behind-the-scenes activities create a climate where teachers feel appreciated for their instructional efforts and can spend the majority of their time doing what they like best—teaching students. These three types of indirect behaviors can assist teachers' instructional efforts:

Acquire resources for teachers. Whenever teachers have to spend time searching for materials, new ideas, or financial resources to attend workshops, they lose valuable time and energy that could be better spent directed toward planning, implementing, and evaluating lessons. Therefore, by being visible and listening to teachers' wishes and concerns, the proactive principal can begin to search for the needed financial and human resources. Principals can become information and resource "brokers" by purchasing instructional materials, building a professional library of readings, locating money to support professional travel, and providing release time for teachers to observe one another and visit other schools. This form of indirect involvement by principals is often viewed by teachers as one of the most meaningful actions principals can do to support their instructional efforts.

Attend to the maintenance of the building. A shabby, unkept school environment communicates to students, teachers, parents, and the community that the school has little regard for their physical safety. A clean and structurally sound school building, however, provides a more inviting atmosphere in which teaching and learning can occur. Besides keeping up the grounds, hallways, and corridors, principals need to maintain classrooms by making sure they are well lit, are free of graffiti, have clean windows, are well ventilated, and have adequate numbers of chairs, desks, and tables that are comfortable and the right size for students.

Assist students in resolving their problems. Disruptive and unhappy students can make life miserable for teachers. Rather than spending their time teaching students, teachers can find themselves attending to behavioral problems that interrupt the flow of classroom events and detract from other students' abilities to concentrate on and participate in learning activities. Although principals should resist solving all the discipline problems teachers face, they can support teachers' classroom practices and school policies by speaking with students and their parents about appropriate classroom demeanor, visiting students in their homes to show their concern, and enforcing school policies regarding vandalism, tardiness, and absenteeism.

The degree to which teachers view principals as credible resources may be determined by using a checklist as shown in Figure 4.1. This checklist of the principal's direct and indirect supportive behavior can be used to ascertain areas of strength and needed improvement.

One way for principals to use such a checklist is to compare their responses to the items with the reactions of teachers. This comparison will allow principals to determine not only areas of agreement, but also areas that may need to be strengthened. If principals are willing to be open and honest regarding teachers' feedback, they might work with a small group of teachers who would be willing to identify ways in which the principal can attend to areas that may be deficient. Such attempts to obtain and respond to teachers' concerns can go a long way toward building the trust and credibility needed to become an effective instructional leader.

Coaching for Professional Development

Deming encourages leaders to be coaches and counselors. The coaching concept has received recent attention in education, especially for classroom teachers. Bruce Joyce and Beverly Showers, two of the earliest proponents of *peer coaching*, contend that as teachers observe and provide feedback to one another they can improve their teaching strategies (Joyce & Showers, 1982; Showers, 1985). A further refinement of the coaching process is *cognitive coaching* (Costa & Garmston, 1985; Tye, Costa, & Garmston, 1986). The distinguishing feature of cognitive coaching is that the principal works closely with teachers to refine their perceptions, decisions, and intellectual functioning. The underlying assumption of cognitive coaching is that if teachers understand how they think about the teaching process, they will be better able to make conscious decisions about how to improve their instructional behaviors and consequently student learning will be positively affected. The ultimate goal of cognitive coaching is to eliminate the principal's involvement so that teachers can become autonomous learners, monitoring their own thought processes and decision-making strategies.

Besides the direct and indirect supportive actions described earlier, the effective instructional leader can ensure higher levels of teacher performance by coaching teachers as well as providing opportunities for other teachers to coach one another. Once teachers understand the underlying assumptions of coaching, the actions that support a true coaching atmosphere can be developed and supported. In this way, principals can establish a culture where teachers feel valued and where teaching is viewed as being integral to the success of all students. In fully understanding the philosophy of coaching and how to be an effective coach and/or how to facilitate the coaching process among the teaching staff, principals must be aware of four important aspects of coaching: (a) the different approaches to coaching, (b) the distinction between coaching and evaluation, (c) the observational and feedback strategies associated with coaching, and (d) the training and support required for peer coaches.

Models of Coaching

As we noted previously, there are various forms of coaching that have been developed. Underlying these different approaches, however, are certain assumptions about what the coaching process is intended to do and how it ought to be conducted. Three approaches described by Garmston (1987) provide an overview of different coaching processes. These approaches or models are referred to as *technical coaching, collegial coaching,* and *challenge coaching*. Following is a brief description as well as highlights of the advantages and disadvantages of each model.

- *Technical coaching.* A process in which teachers observe one another and provide feedback as a peer attempts to put into practice a particular skill or approach introduced in a workshop or in-service training session.

(Text continues on page 80)

	Strongly Agree	Agree	Disagree	Strongly Disagree
Direct Behaviors				
The principal frequently observes teachers' classrooms.	1	2	3	4
The principal provides helpful feedback and suggestions during postconferences.	1	2	3	4
The principal shares ideas about effective instruction and student assessment.	1	2	3	4
The principal assists faculty in interpreting students' test results.	1	2	3	4
The principal helps teachers determine how the district's goals link to their classroom goals.	1	2	3	4
The principal provides opportunities for teachers to engage in staff development activities.	1	2	3	4
The principal supports teachers who work collaboratively to improve their instruction and to create teaching materials and activities.	1	2	3	4
The principal leads formal and informal discussions about instruction.	1	2	3	4
The principal communicates a clear vision for where the school is headed.	1	2	3	4

Figure 4.1. Checklist of the Principal's Direct and Indirect Supportive Behaviors

	Strongly Agree	Agree	Disagree	Strongly Disagree
The principal provides ongoing feedback to teachers regarding their classroom performance.	1	2	3	4
The principal communicates effectively through written and verbal communications.	1	2	3	4
The principal is an active participant in staff development.	1	2	3	4
The principal is a visible presence throughout the school building.	1	2	3	4

Indirect Behaviors

	Strongly Agree	Agree	Disagree	Strongly Disagree
The principal obtains instructional materials for teachers to improve their teaching.	1	2	3	4
The principal locates financial resources to support teachers' professional development.	1	2	3	4
The principal minimizes interruptions during teachers' classroom instruction.	1	2	3	4
The principal provides release time for teachers to observe one another, visit other schools, or attend staff development activities.	1	2	3	4

(Continued)

80 ✧ The TQE Principal: A Transformed Leader

	Strongly Agree	Agree	Disagree	Strongly Disagree
The principal works to maintain the physical appearance of the school building and grounds.	1	2	3	4
The principal provides classrooms with needed chairs, desks, and instructional supplies.	1	2	3	4
The principal makes sure classrooms are well lit and ventilated.	1	2	3	4
The principal supports teachers' classroom discipline practices.	1	2	3	4
The principal communicates behavioral and academic expectations to students and parents.	1	2	3	4
The principal enforces school policies regarding vandalism, tardiness, and absenteeism.	1	2	3	4

Figure 4.1. Continued

Goals: This approach is intended to transfer the information from the workshop setting into practice, to enhance teacher collegiality, to increase professional dialogue, and to create a shared vocabulary.

Advantages: Teaching strategies are used more effectively, knowledge and skills are retained, and the purposes and uses of particular skills are better understood.

Disadvantages: A large time investment is required, release time is needed, the possibility of evaluation can emerge, and defensiveness can occur.
- *Collegial coaching.* A process in which teachers determine an area for self-improvement and have a colleague observe and provide feedback.

  Goals: This process is meant to refine current teaching practices, to increase collegiality, to promote professional dialogue, and to encourage self-reflection.

  Advantages: Teachers' self-concepts are improved, they have a greater sense of efficacy, and they are more open to change.

  Disadvantages: A large investment of time is required, release time is needed, and the desired effects may not be realized immediately.
- *Challenge coaching.* A process in which teams of teachers meet to discuss problems, challenge one another to create possible solutions to problems, and attempt the solutions posed.

  Goals: This approach strives to improve teaching practices, to strengthen collegiality, and to create norms that support professional dialogue.

  Advantages: Solutions to persistent problems are developed and more staff are involved in planning and implementing school improvement efforts.

  Disadvantages: Release time is required, a facilitator with knowledge of group processing and effective teaching strategies is needed, and the investment of time may not result in immediate effects.

These approaches indicate that coaching need not always involve the direct observation of teachers' classroom performance, refuting a common perception held by many people about the coaching process. The key aspect of coaching is that teaching methods become the focus of the discussion, with some commitment and follow-through to act. For instance, technical and collegial coaching require teachers to observe one another; however, challenge coaching allows teachers to report what they are doing to their peers, rather than having teachers visit and observe classrooms.

Furthermore, principals can support and become directly involved in all of these models. Although principals would not be likely to engage in technical coaching because they do not teach separate groups of students, they can provide the resources (e.g., money to attend workshops; substitutes to cover classes during workshop attendance, classroom observation, and feedback sessions) needed to allow teachers to participate. Principals can engage in collegial and challenge coaching; however, if these approaches are to be directed by teachers, then principals must not force themselves on teachers, but wait to be asked to participate.

There are certain trade-offs to using these different approaches that should be seriously considered prior to embarking on a formal coaching program. Technical and collegial coaching may well establish stronger collegial bonds between teachers, but many teachers are apprehensive about having other teachers observe them, especially if they have little or no say in who will be their peer partner. Also, to expect teachers to begin technical or collegial coaching without some training can be a major mistake. (A description of a training system for teachers and principals is presented later in this chapter.) The time for training and engaging in the coaching process requires a substantial time commitment from teachers as well as the financial resources to support the necessary release time. Finally, the time required to learn about, practice, and refine their coaching skills can be substantial. Madeline Hunter, for example, estimates that it can take teachers up to 50 hours of classroom observation before they fully realize the benefits of peer coaching. Principals who are considering peer coaching need not only realize the importance of these time commitments but also must secure the resources needed to release teachers from their teaching responsibilities. This may require hiring substitutes, having principals and other administrators cover classes, or reducing the teaching loads of certain teachers to become coaches.

Coaching Versus Evaluation

Because many teachers have little experience with coaching, there is a tendency to confuse it with the evaluation processes teachers experience in working with principals and other administrators. A key distinction between evaluation and coaching is who is in control of the information being collected and how this information is being used to improve the teaching process. When teachers are evaluated by administrators they have little input about the standards or criteria they are being judged against. Typically, school districts develop formal evaluation instruments that dictate the types of information (e.g., classroom management skills, organizational skills, punctuality) on which administrators are to judge teachers. During coaching, however, teachers control what information is being collected by specifying what area(s) they would like some help in improving. This notion of self-determination corresponds to the collegial and challenge coaching approaches identified earlier. The major differences in coaching and evaluation are underscored in Figure 4.2.

Observation and Feedback Strategies

The qualified coach needs to be well versed in making classroom observations and in providing useful feedback to teachers. This is true if a principal is coaching teachers or teachers are coaching one another. In order to be viewed as credible classroom observers, coaches must have a variety of observational strategies they can use or refine depending on the types of feedback desired by the observed teacher. Coaches should not guess what feedback or input teachers want; they must listen carefully to the observed teacher prior to the observation so they can clarify what the lesson is attempting to accomplish and what specific feedback would be helpful. As Figure 4.2 shows, taking this nonjudgmental stance as a coach allows the observed teacher to determine what information is of most importance to his or her improvement. More will be said later in this chapter about how the discussions during preconference and postconference sessions can assist in clarifying the goals of the coaching process and in altering the process to meet the needs of the observed teacher.

Although there are a variety of classroom observation strategies that have been implemented, the Association for Supervision and Curriculum Development (1987) has summarized six techniques that can serve a variety of purposes. These strategies include:

	Coaching	Evaluation
Purpose:	Teachers sharing their craft and knowledge to provide one another with professional companionship, feedback, and support to refine present skills and learn new ones	Certifying the teacher's competence that can be presented to the school board, public, and staff
Climate:	Safe environment to experiment, fail, revise, and try again	Try only well-developed practices that ensure the teacher's best performance
Timing:	Formative—throughout the year	Summative—near the end of the year
Topics covered:	Determined by inviting teacher: classroom practices, questioning strategies, instructional effectiveness	Determined by administrator and/or school district: involvement in school events, subject matter coverage, punctuality
Value judgments:	Made by the inviting teacher	Made by the administrator
Observer's role:	Directed by the inviting teacher	Determined by the administrator
Power:	Bestowed by the inviting teacher	Bestowed by the school board, administrator, and state
Feedback:	Developed by and for both the teacher and coach	Given only by the administrator to the teacher
Interaction:	Active involvement of teacher and coach	Active involvement of only the administrator
Communication:	Problem solving, mutual inquiry, two-way communcation	Reporting, documenting, one-way communication

Figure 4.2. Major Differences in the Coaching and Evaluation Processes

- Selective verbatim: A written record of the exact words used by students or the teacher is obtained. Rather than recording all verbal interactions, the focus of the observation might be on the questions a teacher asks, the responses of certain students, or the questions students pose to one another.
- Verbal flow: Using a seating chart, the observer indicates who initiates a communication and who responds. This technique provides information about how often students are involved in classroom discussions.
- At task: The observer records the level of engagement of individual students throughout a class lesson. These engagement levels are determined by the observed teacher during a preconference and might include "off task," "doing assigned work," and "waiting for the teacher."
- Class traffic: As the observed teacher moves around the room, the observer notes where the teacher goes, with which students he or she interacts, and how long these interactions last.
- Interaction analysis: Different types of verbal behavior expressed by teachers and students are recorded. Teachers' interactions might include "praising or encouraging," "asking questions," or "lecturing"; student interactions might consist of "responding to questions," "asking questions," or "initiating a discussion."
- Global scan: General information about the classroom is collected using anecdotal notes, audiotapes, or videotapes. This scan of the classroom provides the teacher with an overall picture of classroom events.

Besides being knowledgeable about the types of information to collect during an observation, coaches and teachers must establish the ground rules for the observation. Coaches must not only meet with teachers prior to the observation to understand what teachers are attempting to accomplish during the lesson and what observational techniques might be most appropriate, but also mutually determine how they should conduct themselves during the observation. The following issues should be addressed and clarified prior to beginning classroom observations:

Time of observation. Coaches should observe class sessions that fit the convenience of the observed teacher. Rather than showing up unannounced, coaches should ask when the teacher wants them to observe and then arrive on time. If, however, coaches arrive at the prearranged time and circumstances have changed due to unforeseen events, then coaches need to be flexible and reschedule at a more convenient time for the observed teacher.

Seating location. Coaches need to locate themselves so they can see and hear what goes on in the classroom without distracting teachers or students. The observed teacher needs to decide the best place(s) for coaches to locate themselves so as not to disrupt classroom events. Being in the direct line of sight of the teacher might make him or her more aware of the coaches' presence; sitting to the side of the classroom might reduce this tendency to make eye contact. In some cases, the observed teacher might decide coaches should move around the room to better hear or see particular events.

Interaction with students. Often students are tempted to interact with coaches during the observation. Students may want help with an assignment, want to know why the coach is there, or want to share an experience with another adult. If coaches are to be unobtrusive, they need to refrain from interacting with students as much as possible. Therefore, coaches need to anticipate students' reactions to their presence, briefly responding when students try to engage them in conversations.

Explanation to students. Just as coaching may be a new experience for teachers, it also may be foreign for students to have another adult in the room recording events. Prior to the first observation, the teacher should explain to students why the coach will be observing, when the coach will be coming, and how the coach is to interact with students during the observation. Typically, this explanation is not enough to satisfy the curiosity of some students; they will still try to converse with coaches during the initial observations. Eventually, if coaches refrain from interacting, students tend to ignore them in subsequent observations.

After having conducted a classroom observation, coaches need to provide nonjudgmental feedback to teachers about what they observed, helping teachers to clarify how well the lesson accomplished its goals and to determine ways they might improve in the future. Although many people perceive feedback as an evaluation of their performance, truly useful feedback implies no judgment, but is a descriptive account of the teacher's observed behavior and classroom events. In attempting to provide useful feedback about a teacher's performance, coaches should keep the following guidelines in mind:

- Provide descriptive feedback, not evaluative judgments. By having observed events described to them, teachers can react to what occurred rather than having to defend or refute an evaluative comment.
- Give specific information about observed events. Recalling the exact words or details of an interaction focuses a teacher's attention on the event, thus avoiding generalities.
- Keep the needs of the teacher in mind. Communication can be hindered if the person sending the feedback pushes his or her viewpoints on the teacher. Therefore, the person providing the feedback must always consider whether the feedback is being asked for or is being imposed.
- Provide feedback as soon as possible. Situations are easier to recall if a substantial amount of time has not passed since they occurred.
- Allow the teacher to focus on behavior over which he or she has control. If a teacher cannot alter an event or personal characteristic, any feedback directed at such issues may provide some insight, but the situation may be unchangeable.

Besides these general guidelines, there are specific types of responses and behaviors coaches can utilize to help facilitate the observed teacher's thinking while maintaining a neutral, nonjudgmental stance. The following summarize the types of actions coaches should be encouraged to use:

- Ask clarifying questions to get the teacher to explain the situation in greater detail, using his or her own language.
- Listen more and talk less to allow the teacher to fully examine the lesson without outside judgment or interference.
- Acknowledge and paraphrase what is heard to make sure there are no misconceptions between what the teacher is expressing and what the coach is hearing.
- Avoid providing direct advice, unless the teacher actively solicits the coach's input.
- Assist teachers to be more precise in their explanations by having them clarify vague verbs, self-imposed rules, over-generalizations, and vague comparisons.
- Allow teachers to accept responsibility for their own actions by having them prescribe their own solutions to problems, choose among possible alternative solutions, and recognize the results of their actions.
- Elicit alternative techniques and explanations by having the teacher consider previous experience in a similar situation, explain how students might view the situation, and determine the possible consequences of different decisions.

Just as coaches and teachers need to consider the logistical considerations for conducting the observation, they need to discuss how and when the feedback should be presented. To be most effective, the feedback should occur as soon as possible and during a time when the teacher can devote full attention to the discussion. To assist teachers in determining how they would like to see this feedback session or postconference conducted, coaches can pose the following questions for teachers to consider prior to the conference:

- When would be a convenient time for me to meet with you to discuss the observation?

- Where should we meet? Your room? My room? Somewhere else here at school? Or would you rather meet somewhere else? Before school at a local restaurant? After school at my house for coffee?
- How would you like me to present the information I collected? Would you like to see my notes before the session?
- I'd also like you to give me some feedback about my role as a coach. What should I continue to do to make this useful for you? What would you like to change for the next observation and feedback sessions?

By openly addressing these issues, the coach is allowing the teacher to determine how to make the feedback session as useful as possible as well as how the process can be improved in the future. Taking such a stance as a coach can help to build a relationship between coaches and teachers that is founded on trust, open communication, and mutual regard.

Training and Support for Coaches

When teachers begin to coach one another there is usually some hesitation and apprehension about taking on this new role. Therefore, when principals consider having teachers coach one another, they need to provide initial training in this new role as well as ongoing support and assistance. Although principals need not conduct the training sessions themselves, they do, however, need to find other teachers or administrators who have experience with the coaching process who can orient teachers to this new role. By locating these resources, principals are providing another form of indirect support for teachers.

What then might this training look like? Figure 4.3 presents an overview of the different components that can be incorporated in a peer coaching training program. An important first step in getting coaches to become more knowledgeable about and comfortable with their peer partners is to have them conduct a *background interview*. This interview provides the coach with important contextual information about the partner's desired learning outcomes for

90 ✧ The TQE Principal: A Transformed Leader

```
┌─────────────────────────────────────────┐
│         Background Interview            │
├─────────────────────────────────────────┤
│ Obtain contextual information about the │
│ teacher's attitudes and classroom       │
│ activities                              │
└─────────────────────────────────────────┘
                    │
                    ▼
┌─────────────────────────────────────────┐
│       Pre-Observation Conference        │
├─────────────────────────────────────────┤
│ Clarify the observation process and     │◄──┐
│ what will be observed during the lesson │   │
└─────────────────────────────────────────┘   │
                    │                         │
                    ▼                         │
┌─────────────────────────────────────────┐   │
│              Observation                │   │
├─────────────────────────────────────────┤   │
│ Gather descriptive information about    │   │
│ the classroom lesson                    │   │
└─────────────────────────────────────────┘   │
           │                                  │
           ▼                                  │
┌──────────────────────┐   ┌──────────────────────────────┐
│ Reflective Conference│   │    Debriefing Conference     │
├──────────────────────┤   ├──────────────────────────────┤
│ Self-examination by  │──▶│ - Determination of strengths │
│ teacher of the       │   │   and areas for future       │
│ events that occurred │   │   improvement                │
│ during the lesson    │   │                              │
│                      │   │ - Determination of how to    │
│                      │   │   alter future observation   │
│                      │   │   and conference sessions    │
└──────────────────────┘   └──────────────────────────────┘
```

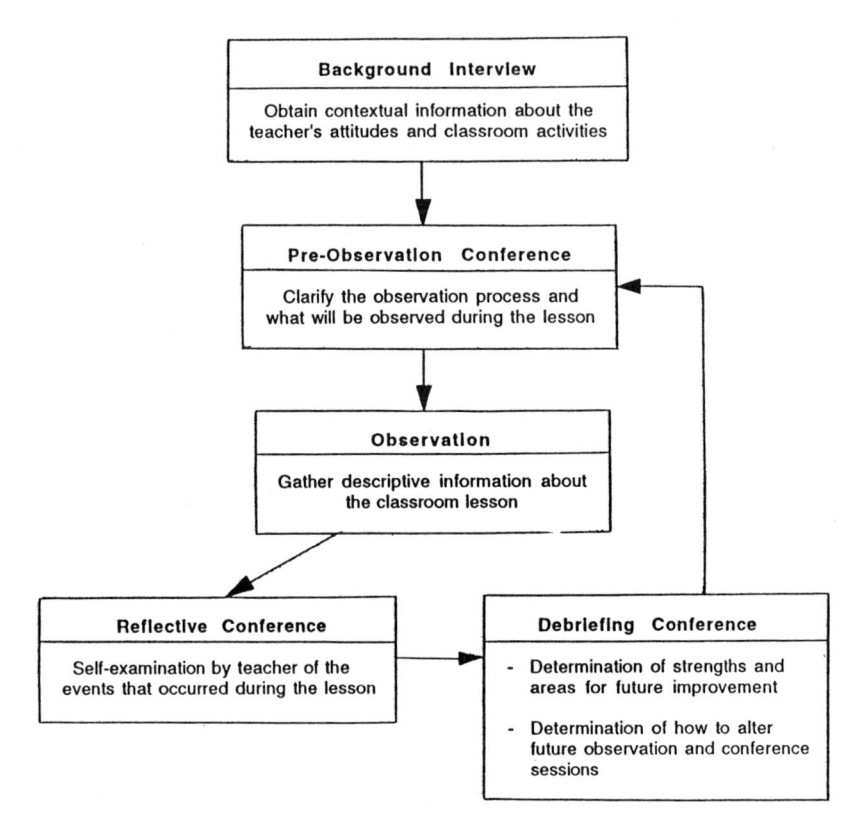

Figure 4.3. Major Components in the Peer Coaching Process

students, classroom procedures and learning activities, and beliefs about children and learning. One approach to conducting this background interview is to have teachers address the seven areas of an educational platform outlined in Figure 1.1. The value of this initial activity is that peer coaches get to know more about one another's professional attitudes and values before beginning the classroom observation phase of the process. By having this information beforehand, coaches are less likely to be judgmental about what they are observing as they already have an understanding of what the teacher values and why certain activities are being used.

After gaining this background information, the coach and observed teacher need to engage in a *preobservation conference* followed by the actual classroom observation. During the preobservation conference coaches need to clarify what the teacher wants feedback about and how they should conduct themselves during the observation. Coaches can suggest various observation techniques they might use, such as selective verbatim, at task, class traffic, or verbal flow. They also need to mutually determine with the observed teacher the ground rules for their involvement. Decisions need to be made concerning the ideas examined earlier about when it is convenient to conduct the observation, where the coach will be located in the classroom, how the coach is to interact with students, and what students will be told about the coach's involvement in the classroom. Once these decisions have been made, the coach conducts the observation, adhering to the ground rules set forth in the preobservation conference.

The final component of the coaching process is the method for providing feedback to the teacher following the observation of the lesson. Figure 4.3 displays this feedback in two parts: the *reflective conference* and the *debriefing conference*. Actually, these are two phases of the same interview session, each with a different purpose. The intent of the reflective interview is for the observed teacher to examine his or her actions, determining the extent to which the planned activities accomplished their intended effects. Besides using the general guidelines for providing useful feedback, the qualified coach incorporates the active listening skills and feedback strategies mentioned above to stimulate the teacher to think about the lesson. Often the observed teacher will solicit the advice or suggestions of the coach about what occurred during the lesson. At this point in the conference, the coach should refrain from giving input, indicating that he or she will gladly react after having heard all that the observed teacher has to say. After the teacher has fully explored his or her actions, the coach moves into the debriefing phase of the conference by: (a) providing suggestions or giving advice about issues the observed teacher raised during the reflective conference and (b) determining what went well in observing and providing feedback and what changes the coach needs to make in the future to make the teacher feel more comfortable. As Figure 4.3 shows, once the debriefing is completed, the teacher and coach are ready for another observation and feedback cycle. In many instances, rather than holding a separate preobservation conference prior to the next cycle, the teacher and coach make the necessary decisions during the debriefing session. Combining these steps does not violate the coaching process, but allows the teacher and coach to use their time more efficiently.

To equip coaches and teachers with the skills necessary to engage in these different components, an orientation session should be conducted that alerts participants to these different components and allows them to practice conducting background interviews, preobservation conferences, observations, reflective conferences, and debriefing conferences. After the initial training and as coaches begin to work with teachers, they need ongoing support and assistance as their collegial interactions unfold. Barnett (1990) suggests coaches and teachers need to meet periodically to discuss their progress. These discussions are meant to acknowledge the joys and frustrations that are being experienced and to help coaches overcome old habits (e.g., being judgmental). These discussions are meant to help coaches and teachers through four phases of the coaching process:

Phase 1: Working on the mechanics. Coaches and teachers need time to become comfortable with the components of this process. Their initial experiences with observations and reflective conferences can be somewhat frustrating because they are trying new skills and behaviors. They need time to work out the bugs in their interactions; hearing how other people are dealing with these same difficulties can be most helpful.

Phase 2: Becoming collegial. Once coaches and teachers begin expressing some comfort with the mechanics of the coaching process, they are better able to focus their future observations and conferences on issues of clear importance to the teacher. In this way, they are moving toward Garmston's (1987) notion of collegial coaching.

Phase 3: Correcting the process. As observations and conferences continue, coaches and teachers need to reflect on whether their interactions are serving their intended purposes. If coaching is not confirming their actions or expanding their repertoire of skills, teachers need to discuss this with the coach to determine what improvements need to be made to make their time expenditure worth the effort.

Phase 4: Summarizing the experience. As coaches and teachers near the end of their experience, they need time to determine how the coaching process has met its original purpose and how they have been personally and professionally affected by the experience. Besides considering the current worth of coaching, participants can determine ways to expand and adjust this process in the future.

Even though their position of authority sometimes inhibits the relationship principals can build with teachers, the transformed principal who follows the TQE adage of being a coach and counselor needs to take a positive, supportive stance in working with teachers. Focusing on the good things that are happening, asking what help teachers need and then finding it, refraining from taking a judgmental approach, and supporting teachers who want to coach one another all contribute to making teachers feel valued and willing to take risks. Building this level of trust with teachers will not happen overnight; principals must be patient and nurture these relationships in small steps. When they do so, the customer at the end of the pipeline is bound to receive and perceive significant benefits.

Key Terms and Concepts

Background interview. An interview or conference held between a coach and a teacher prior to beginning the peer coaching process. The intent of this discussion is for the coach to get a better understanding of the observed teacher's beliefs, values, desired student outcomes, classroom rules, and instructional activities.

Challenge coaching. Groups of teachers and/or administrators who meet periodically to discuss problems and whose members challenge the group to brainstorm possible solutions. The expectation is that teachers and administrators must report at subsequent meetings how the solutions they have been implementing are working.

Coaching. An improvement strategy whereby teachers receive guidance and feedback about their teaching from a coach who usually observes their classroom teaching. This approach emphasizes that teachers determine their own needs rather than having someone else's rules or standards imposed on them.

Cognitive coaching. A process of feedback in which teachers examine the thought processes that guide their decisions about teaching. The ultimate goal is for teachers to independently assess their thinking without the intervention of another person.

Collegial coaching. Teachers determine what they would like a coach to observe them doing in their classroom for purposes of their own self-growth and improvement.

Debriefing conference. A component in the coaching process during which the coach and teacher determine what is going well in their relationship, what needs to be altered, and what the teacher might do to improve future lessons.

Direct supportive behaviors. Actions principals can take to support teachers' instructional efforts that include making frequent classroom observations, facilitating staff development programs, constantly communicating with teachers about instructional matters, and being visible throughout the school building and grounds.

Evaluation. The process of determining whether teachers have met an acceptable standard of performance. Typically, teachers have little say or control over evaluation; the principal or another administrator makes the final decision about their competence.

Feedback strategies. Specific actions taken by a person to provide helpful guidance and support to another person without judging or evaluating performance. Feedback is most useful when it is specific, timely, and nonjudgmental and when it allows the recipient to examine the reasons behind his or her actions.

Indirect supportive behaviors. The behind-the-scenes activities principals can do to support teachers' instructional efforts. This includes acquiring resources, attending to the maintenance of the building and grounds, and assisting students in resolving their classroom and nonacademic difficulties.

Observation strategies. Techniques used by a classroom observer to collect information about classroom events, such as teaching behaviors and materials, student attention, and student-teacher interactions.

Preobservation conference. A conference held between a coach and teacher prior to the classroom observation. This conference provides the opportunity for the observed teacher to clarify the goals and activities of the lesson and for both of them to determine the ground rules for the coach's involvement in the classroom.

Reflective conference. Following the observation, the coach provides the teacher with nonjudgmental feedback about what was observed during the lesson. The purpose is to get the teacher to engage in self-examination rather than have the coach decide what went well or poorly during the lesson.

Technical coaching. An observation and feedback process used when teachers are attempting to try a new skill introduced in a workshop setting. The intent is to help the teacher transfer what he or she learned from the workshop setting into the classroom with the guidance of a coach.

References

Association for Supervision and Curriculum Development. (1987). *Another set of eyes: Techniques for classroom observation* [Trainer's manual]. Alexandria, VA: Author.
Barnett, B. G. (1990). Overcoming obstacles to peer coaching for principals. *Educational Leadership, 47,* 62-64.

Costa, A. L., & Garmston, R. (1985). Supervision for intelligent teaching. *Educational Leadership, 42,* 70-80.

Frase, L. E. (1992). *Maximizing people power in schools: Motivating and managing teachers and staff.* Newbury Park, CA: Corwin.

Garmston, R. (1987). How administrators support peer coaching. *Educational Leadership, 44,* 18-26.

Joyce, B., & Showers, B. (1982). The coaching of teaching. *Educational Leadership, 40,* 4-10.

Liu, C. J. (1984). *An identification of principals' instructional leadership in effective high schools.* Unpublished doctoral dissertation. Cincinnati: University of Cincinnati.

Showers, B. (1985). Teachers coaching teachers. *Educational Leadership, 42,* 43-48.

Smith, W. F., & Andrews, R. L. (1989). *Instructional leadership: How principals make a difference.* Alexandria, VA: Association for Supervision and Curriculum Development.

Sparks, D., & Loucks-Horsley, S. (1989). Five models of staff development for teachers. *Journal of Staff Development, 10,* 40-54.

Tye, K., Costa, A., & Garmston, R. (1986). *Better teaching through instructional supervision: Policy and practice.* Sacramento: California School Boards Association.

✧ 5 ✧

Making Quality Decisions Based on Data

It is important to remember that the TQM movement grew out of a statistician's view of management. Recently, quantitative measurement in education has developed a bad reputation. Educators often assume that reducing anything to a quantitative bottom line must be inherently reductionist. In fact, some of the language that Deming uses when discussing statistical calculation almost seems to have been chosen to purposefully alienate educators. However, when a proper and sensitive use of statistical tools is understood, they will play more of a liberating function than a restricting one.

The Concept of Reducing Variation

Deming argues that one of the purposes of TQM is to reduce "variation in output." The images that this conjures up for most school people is nothing short of reactionary. That is because educators are used to measuring inputs (students) and are all well aware that one of the glorious things about students is their diversity. The reduced variation that Deming is referring to is variation in outputs. This brings to mind one of the valuable slogans from special education: "There is nothing quite as unfair as treating unequals equally." In no way does TQE contradict this! In the area of systemic process control, what TQE leaders want to accomplish is a modification of the system of throughputs so that despite a wide variety of inputs (student characteristics), through the application of appropriate interventions (the educational process), they are able to achieve universally high quality outputs (student learning).

Some of the pictures encountered in a TQM text look strikingly similar to the bell curves at which educators have grown increasingly tired of looking. After all, the most familiar bell-shaped curve serves to predict (or justify) a world of educational outputs with great variation.

Suppose that a student's academic performance places him at point A. Furthermore, this level of performance enables him to follow directions and execute job expectations for most of the intellectual and practical challenges that would likely be faced by a high school graduate. However, also assume the belief (belief systems were discussed in chapter 1) that a graduate should have skills akin to those possessed by a student performing at point B. In reality these are the skills expected of a student who plans to matriculate at and be successful in a baccalaureate granting institution. For those reasons it is appropriate to call such a level of performance (point B) the desirable (or in Deming's terms, optimal) output. It is desirable because a belief system holds that performing at that level will make a graduate eligible for the entire range of opportunities that society has to offer. In short, if graduates are eligible for college admission, then they have gained entry to the starting line for all professional work. Conversely, any student who falls short of that level of achievement will be restricted to much more limited adult opportunities.

Now let's examine the variation typically found around this desirable/optimal performance point. Most students will fall short of that level of performance. In fact, if the distribution of performance occurs as illustrated in the traditional bell curve, then most of the students attending school will fall short of this optimal output. But a high-performing, TQE-orientated school will seek to alter its systems to reduce this variability of output. The outcome that such a school would want to produce is a distribution of performance that looks more like the one illustrated in Figure 5.1.

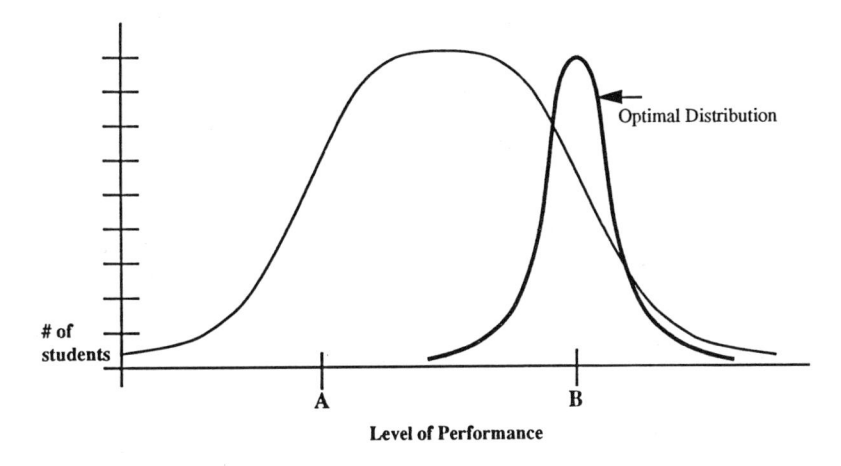

Figure 5.1. Reduced Variability Curve

One goal of the instructional leader is to utilize basic statistical tools to assist the staff in reducing the variability of outputs around whatever point of performance the school community considers optimal. Statistical calculations can serve both managerial as well as motivational purposes. The prime managerial purpose is providing motivated workers with feedback on organizational performance so that adjustments can be made to improve the output. Consider the example of the highly motivated track athlete and his or her coaches (Sagor, 1991). How long would either athlete or coach continue to persevere if he or she were required to practice or compete without the benefit of measuring tape and stopwatches? We suspect it would not be for long. Precise measurements of desired performance (measured against past performance and personal goals) enables athletes or coaches to see when they are achieving consistency, when they are meeting or exceeding personal expectations, and how far they are from becoming truly competitive. School faculties are no different. The measuring and celebrating of success can provide workers in a demanding pursuit (like teaching) a great deal of satisfaction and pride.

The other purpose is a psychological and motivational one. Peter Senge (1990) speaks about the important role for leadership of generating and managing *creative tension* as a mechanism for promoting high levels of performance and encouraging continuous improvement. Briefly put, creative tension is what is felt when a person sees or experiences the difference between the current state of affairs and the optimum level of performance the person wants to achieve. A strategic use of statistical tools can enable the instructional leader to generate creative tension for those being led. This concept is discussed at greater length in the discussion on the management of cognitive dissonance in chapter 6.

The School Profile

As previously mentioned, creative tension is produced when the discrepancy between a current state and a desired or optimal state is acknowledged. As a result the first challenge before the effective principal is to have an accurate statistical picture of the current state. These pictures have become a key feature of the school improvement efforts that had their genesis in the "effective schools" movement. These statistical portraits are frequently called *school profiles*. To be helpful a profile must be comprehensive, possess face validity, and provide data on performance in relation to critical performance targets.

The actual components of a profile should be dictated by the outcomes the school seeks to accomplish and the aspirations embodied in the school's mission statement or vision of excellence. As idiosyncratic as profiles can be, it will, nonetheless, be helpful to review a list of elements that are common to many good profiles. Although schools differ somewhat in the outcomes they seek to achieve, it is the rare school that doesn't endeavor to improve performance in three areas: academic skills, social skills, and responsible behavior. Figure 5.2 lists the items most frequently found in school profiles.

Figures 5.3 and 5.4 are examples of items drawn from profiles developed as part of the "Onward to Excellence Program" of the Northwest Regional Educational Laboratory (NWREL, 1989).

The analysis of the profile is one of the most important tasks undertaken by a school faculty seeking to engage in continuous

Academic Achievement	Social Behavior	Student Attitude
Basic Skills	**Attendance**	**Self as learner**
Standardized test scores in reading, language arts, and math	Attendance information	Standardized measures
	Punctuality	Locally developed measures
	Tardiness information	**School as place to learn**
Criterion-referenced test scores in reading, language arts, and math	**Discipline**	Standardized measures
	Referral information	Locally developed measures
	Vandalism reports	
Performance test in writing	**Responsibility**	
	Assignment completion rate	
Grades in required subjects	Information from deportment section of the report card	
Other subjects		
Standardized test scores		
Criterion-referenced test scores		
Grades in nonrequired subjects		
Excellence		
Scores from standardized measures of higher level thinking		
Grades in advanced cources in all subject areas		
Awards for outstanding performance given by agencies external to the school		

Figure 5.2. Possible Items for Profiles

improvement. When done purposefully and when attention is paid to potential pitfalls, the profile can serve to focus effort, build commitment, and provide motivation. If managed poorly, it may

	Behavior	1985-86	1986-87	1987-88
1.	Alcohol	10	8	16
2.	Assault	15	10	4
3.	Bus	30	31	10
4.	Cheating	6	4	5
5.	Defiance	196	177	273
6.	Disruption	550	529	467
7.	Drugs	7	5	0
8.	Explosives	2	3	28
9.	Fighting	24	26	28
10.	Loitering	23	20	25
11.	Tardiness	1767	1746	1590
12.	Theft	10	11	3
13.	Tobacco	90	83	61
14.	Unexcused	152	133	0
15.	Vandalism	27	23	17
16.	Weapon	18	16	2
	Total students	637	642	634

Figure 5.3. Example of School Profile (Conduct Violations)

do just the opposite, that is, encourage goal displacement, factionalism, and defeatism. It is for these reasons that the skill of the principal as an instructional leader is absolutely critical when the faculty analyze their profile.

The key to profile analysis is to conduct it from a systems perspective. As chapters 1 and 2 discussed and Figure 1.1 visually represented, examining organizational effectiveness through a systems lens allows school professionals to hold the belief that performance can always be improved, all the while avoiding the blaming game. When conducting a systems analysis three components of the production process must be kept in mind: inputs, throughputs, and outputs. If the goal is producing optimal quality, it is imperative to be absolutely clear on the desired outputs (or learnings). Closer examination of Figure 1.1 reveals that inputs include the community, beliefs and experiences, and the institutional context; throughputs consist of the routine behaviors, school climate, and instructional organization; and outputs are the desired student outcomes.

STANDARDIZED TESTS
Reading

Prologue

The data shown below represent the pattern of student performance in reading as measured by the CTBS test. Testing was done in the spring of each year. Tests were administered to all students in grades 2-6.

Data Display

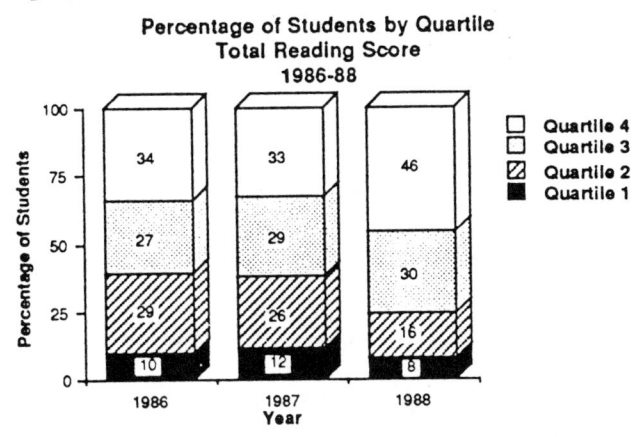

Percentage of Students by Quartile
Total Reading Score
1986-88

Year	Quartile 1	Quartile 2	Quartile 3	Quartile 4
1986	10	29	27	34
1987	12	26	29	33
1988	8	16	30	46

Narratives

- In reading, the percentage of students in the top Quartile (Q4) decreased from 34% in 1986 to 33% in 1987, and then increased to 46% in 1988.
- In reading, the percentage of students in the bottom Quartile (Q1) increased from 10% in 1986 to 12% in 1987, and then decreased to 8% in 1988.
- Over the three year period (86-88) in reading, the percentage of students above the national norm, 50th percentile, increased from 61 to 76 percent.

Figure 5.4. Example of School Profile (Standardized Tests)

STP Charts

One approach used for profile analysis is the *STP chart*. This was not named for the popular oil additive—rather the STP chart is an analytic device that has proven itself useful for the management of creative tension. The columns of the chart stand for *situation*, *target*, and *proposal*. We suggest that one begins the analysis with the middle column (target). It is here that the faculty concisely and clearly lists the specific optimal performances it wishes to achieve in a particular content area. For example, assume that a faculty decided to pursue the outcome of helping students become self-directed learners. Furthermore, assume that this faculty articulated an expectation that in a successful school that was pursuing that goal, each student would complete at least three multidisciplinary projects of their own choosing each school year. Finally, assume that the faculty clearly defined a set of assessment criteria that could be used to determine if individual projects met that standard.

In such a school the profile would be expected to contain data on the achievement of this self-directed learner "target" by the student body. Data such as percentage of students completing three projects and the percentage of projects that met or exceeded the performance criteria would be collected and reported. This data would then be summarized in the first column of the chart. The first two columns of Figure 5.5 show how an STP chart from this school would look at this point in the process. Typically this would have been prepared and exhibited on a large piece of butcher paper in a faculty meeting.

Once the first two columns have been completed, the group is ready to be led through the process of systems thinking. Specifically they would need to ask themselves:

- What factors (within our span of control) could be influencing the discrepancy between what we desire (the optimum) and what we are achieving?
- What are some of the possible changes we can make in our system that will have an impact on the outputs of this system?

These should be discussed openly with an attitude seeking not to assign blame, but to build understanding. Group members should be asked to critique proposals that emerge at this stage in an effort to surface pilot (experimental) projects with a potential

Situation	Target	Proposal
57% of the students are completing three projects that meet the criteria.	Each student will complete at least three multidisciplinary projects of his or her own choosing each year.	1. A mentoring system will be established so each student will have a "faculty guide." 2. Curriculum revisions will be made in core disciplines to stress interrelationships. 3. Scoring rubrics will be created to assist students with self-assessment.

Figure 5.5. STP chart

for reducing the gap between current and optimal levels of performance. If ideas meet the initial test of reasonableness, then they can be placed in the third column (proposals).

The key thing that a leader needs to do at this stage is to be certain that all members of the team understand what placement of a proposition in the proposal column means. Being written there does not mean that this proposal is now policy. Rather, placement in that column denotes only that some members of the team believe that there is merit in exploring these particular throughput processes. This translates to an acceptance of the proposition that "some reasonable people have reason to suspect that these changes in process will lead to desirable changes in output." This understanding is imperative because the next stage for leadership will be soliciting volunteers who want to work out the breakthroughs needed to test these assumptions. If instead a leader allowed these proposals to be classified as "truths" (such as the ones found on stone tablets on Mt. Sinai), it would be unlikely that anyone would be willing to invest energy, or worse, assume personal risk in their attainment. The goal for the instructional leader is to encourage folks with both high standards and a commitment to certain propositions to invest their energy (without fear of failure) in the pursuit of reasoned experimentation. A completed STP chart might look like the one exhibited in Figure 5.5.

Collaborative Action Research

The following discussion was adopted from *How to Conduct Collaborative Action Research* (Sagor, 1993). One valuable method for institutionalizing system thinking and taking advantage of creative tension in a school is through the practice of *collaborative action research*. Collaborative action research is a strategy that when properly implemented tends to make teaching more like other (higher status) professions in several key ways.

*Teachers Work in Isolation
From Other Professionals*

Although teaching may not be the world's "oldest" profession, it certainly is one of the world's loneliest. All one needs to do is shadow a doctor, lawyer, engineer, or architect for a day and it becomes obvious that they spend far more time with their colleagues than they do with clients. A doctor frequently ponders the meaning of an X ray with other physicians and health care workers, a lawyer may consult with associates on trial strategy, and engineers and architects will work in teams to develop new prototypes and designs. These professional-to-professional interactions stimulate and push practitioners to new levels of performance in both the art and craft of their profession.

Contrast this with the world inhabited by the typical classroom teacher. The teacher role in America is not unlike a group of preschoolers engaged in "parallel play" (Barth, 1987). Although they may work in a building with other teachers and even use the same materials and follow the same schedule, one rarely sees two teachers conversing with each other during the student contact day except during their 30-minute duty-free lunch period (where informal norms frequently make professional talk verboten). This dearth of collegial stimulation would be bad enough if teaching were a profession with a certain and finite knowledge base. But because it is a field that mixes art with craft and it is a profession in which finding concise definitive solutions to ever-changing and mutating problems is impossible, the isolation of practitioners from meaningful discourse with other professionals can have disastrous effects.

If this continues, inquisitive and collaborative educators can be expected to exit teaching and many who stay with it will stick with simple and easy-to-administer teaching methods. Furthermore, due to this isolated nature of teaching many practitioners will continue to teach with their doors shut for fear of exposing to colleagues that they have not yet mastered this "unmasterable" craft.

Generation of Knowledge

All professions are informed by a knowledge base. Teaching is no exception, with a body of accepted research literature on effective teaching practices and successful schooling techniques. As in other professions, educational practitioners are expected to be familiar with, make use of, and respect the foundations of their practice. But that is not all that is expected. In all of the professions except teaching, practitioners are also expected to interact with and contribute to the development of their profession's knowledge base.

Pick up any medical journal and one will find that most of the articles are written by practicing physicians. The formats are remarkably similar. The author first explains what problems were manifest by their patients and then details the treatments that were employed. The author/physician concludes by sharing the results obtained by the treatment of the patients. The function of this medical literature and expanding knowledge base is to alert other physicians to what colleagues are learning. A doctor reads such articles all the while asking: (a) Are my patients demonstrating similar needs? and (b) If yes, should I attempt similar interventions?

Similarly, the knowledge base of engineers is the work of other engineers. Each one, like Copernicus, sits on the shoulders of giants (their colleagues and peers), whose work informs the next generation of innovation. Architects draw plans based on the work of other architects, and lawyers construct briefs and legal arguments based on the experience of other lawyers. Contrast this with the profession of teaching.

Educational journals generally do not feature the work of teachers; rather they serve as vehicles for the dissemination of ideas, commentaries, and studies from people (professors, consultants, administrators) who work outside the classroom world. The topics, problems, or issues pursued are the ones that these outside observers see as significant, not necessarily the problems that are most perplexing for the teacher on the front line. The context of the interventions reported or discussed in journals and that compose the knowledge base may or may not conform to the realities of the public school classroom. In education the worlds of research and practice not only are separate but exist in a hierarchy. The teacher who ignores research is likely seen as anti-intellectual or unprofessional.

Finally, traditional policy makers and supervisors demand that teachers implement this externally derived educational research in their work. The prevailing paradigm in education is one of supervisors telling workers how to do their work because of their superior knowledge. This model is not without precedent. In fact, it is the very model of blue-collar work. The foreman always knows best. The line worker's job is simply to follow the manual and meet the boss's expectations. The TQM literature reflects that this approach is increasingly seen as problematic in the trades, but it is clearly disastrous for endeavors thought of as professional. Until or unless teachers become involved in generating the knowledge that informs their practice they will stay cast as subordinate workers rather than empowered professionals.

Separation of Quality Control

In most professions standards of excellence emerge from the profession itself. The work of the master establishes the target for others that follow. Furthermore, monitoring of the bottom line is seen as necessary for maintaining a professional edge. As a consequence of self-monitoring, professionals set their own improvement agendas. Doctors and lawyers examine the results of their work and the needs of their clients and determine where their professional development energies should be placed. Architects and engineers study the designs that are working best and that provide the greatest efficiency and thereby decide where to place their focus for improvement. In short, in most professions the person doing the work is also the one assessing the work. Not so with teaching!

With public school teaching (as on the assembly line) the quality control officer is someone above and apart from the practitioner. In the case of school systems, data on performance is assembled, assessed, and analyzed at levels far removed from the student-teacher interface. A state legislature or a school board often analyzes the previous year's CTBS test and then prescribes an improvement agenda for the state's or district's teachers. Alternatively, a principal might reflect on his or her perceptions of the teaching performance at the school and then prescribe something like "ITIP," "effective schooling," or "outcome-based education" as "just what the faculty needs." Once again, the external environment dictates what should occur in schools.

TQM is based on an assumption that there is no accountability system as powerful as self-regulation. Self-set standards are invariably higher than those set by others. But when working in systems where supervisors are setting the standards, people are often inclined to passively resist or to negatively sanction "rate-busting" peers.

In the school business the operative rule is that "he who controls the data, controls the agenda." If data on performance are the sole bailiwick of those outside the classroom, it is they who will decide on the pertinent issues and based on those issues the data to be collected. Based on that data they will be free to impose improvement agendas on classroom teachers. Absent of any alternative and compelling data set of their own, the classroom teachers will have no option but to remain subject to the "superior" data of their supervisors. As long as teaching remains a profession where isolation is the norm, where the knowledge that informs practice keeps coming from outside the classroom, and where the quality control officers are removed from the classroom, teaching will remain more like a blue-collar job than an intellectual professional pursuit.

This is not mere speculation. As chapter 3 discussed briefly, Judith Warren Little (1982) examined schools that were instructionally more effective and found that certain cultural norms tended to prevail in those schools. For example, she found that in the more successful schools teachers were more likely to have discussions on teaching and learning, to critique one another's work, to collaborate on the preparation of materials, and to jointly prepare lessons. She concluded that the twin norms of collegiality and experimentation were essential ingredients of the work culture of effective schools.

A recent summary of the research on effective school cultures listed 12 norms that distinguished schools in which student growth and development were likely to occur:

1. Collegiality
2. Experimentation
3. High expectations
4. Trust and confidence
5. Tangible support
6. Reaching out to the knowledge bases
7. Appreciation and recognition
8. Caring, celebration, and humor
9. Involvement in decision making
10. Protection of what's important
11. Traditions
12. Honest, open communications (Saphier & King, 1985)

The collaborative action research process is a technique that can foster the very norms that Little, Saphier, and King found to be essential.

The Essence of Collaborative Action Research

The three words in the heading—*collaborative, action,* and *research*—tell most of the story. To encourage teachers to do this work, we will first look at what distinguishes collaborative action research from what most have experienced as empirical educational research in the past.

Collaborative. There is nothing that precludes someone from privately conducting action research. In fact, most action research historically has been conducted by teachers in isolation. For example, if you recall the first day of student teaching, the day when you first designed and executed a lesson, you were doing classical action research. First, you approached the lesson with a hypothesis on how best to teach some particular material to a specified group of children. You then collected data. During the instructional act you watched the students' faces for clues as to how well the instruction was being received, you walked around the desks during independent practice to see how well the students were progressing, and finally you reviewed their tests or quizzes to ascertain what they learned. You concluded your research by evaluating all these data and drawing conclusions about how you might teach this material differently should the opportunity occur in the future.

The above example contains almost all the elements of a full action research study, minus a plan to write up and share the results. Undoubtedly, by continuing to use that type of disciplined inquiry regarding all teaching, all teachers would have become more thoughtful and better educators. Unfortunately, all the reflection in the world will not alter one of the critical elements of the context of teaching—its awesome isolation! It is for this reason that the collaborative action research process is based on teams of practitioners (who share the same work group, be it grade level, department, or school program) working jointly on their inquiries.

Action. Traditionally, "scientific" research is conducted by professional full-time researchers. Scientists generally study the lives or work of others (be they laboratory rats, natives of New Guinea, or classroom teachers), they choose their topics based on their personal predilections or the preference of journal editors, and they publish their work in the hope that someone will someday make use of it. If no one uses their research that is not the researchers' fault, because once they published their report, their work was complete.

Action research on the other hand is conducted by and for the people doing the work. The purpose of action research is to improve one's own action (practice). If others read it, notice it, or make use of it, then that is icing on the cake. The action researcher undertakes a study in order to find out how he or she (the supplier) can do something that the customer values in a better fashion.

There are three types of interrelated action on which educational action researchers often want to focus:

- Initiating action (for example, adopting a text, choosing an alternative assessment strategy). This generally focuses on inputs.
- Monitoring and adjusting action (for example, seeing how a pilot project is proceeding, assessing the early progress of a new program, improving a current practice). This generally focuses on throughputs.
- Evaluating action (for example, preparing a final report on a completed project). This generally focuses on outputs.

When conducting an inquiry in order to initiate action, one is seeking understanding. This type of action research may be classified as "research for action." Similarly when the purpose is to monitor work to improve performance, one is engaging in what could be classified as "research in action." Finally, if the effort is to evaluate work that has been concluded it could be called "research of action."

Research. Research is a word applied to any effort at disciplined inquiry. Many have been schooled in the notion that only investigations that could be reduced to numbers qualify as research. All action research shares in common the focus on phenomena that the supplier wishes to understand better and as a consequence the researchers employ systematic processes to acquire valid and reliable data on those phenomena to improve their products or outputs. In the collaborative action research process the focus of the research is defined by the practitioners (suppliers) themselves.

Overview of the Five-Step Process

The process of collaborative action research has five sequential components: problem formulation, data collection, data analysis, reporting, and action planning.

Problem formulation. This process assists the action researcher to identify issues or areas involved in teaching/learning that are of the greatest professional concern. It helps researchers focus on what they already know about an area of deep concern, what they still need to know about that area, and their understanding of the issues/variables impacting that phenomenon. This is often accomplished by strategies such as journal writing, reflective interviewing, and peer coaching. The problem formulation process also includes constructing a graphic representation of the phenomenon and drafting a focused and concise written problem statement.

Data collection. The second step of collaborative action research, data collection, lies at the heart of the five-step process. The credibility of any research effort lives or dies on the quality of the data used to support its conclusions. To ensure adequate data collection action researchers, their colleagues, students, and significant others are expected to assemble three sets of data for each of the research questions surfaced during the problem formulation phase. This is called triangulation. Sources of data used by teams of action researchers frequently include classroom observations, videotapes, student work, tests, portfolios, checklists, questionnaires, interviews, school records, and student and teacher journals. Experienced action researchers have found that their school buildings are truly data-rich environments.

Data analysis. If data collection is the heart of the research process, then data analysis is its soul. Most action researchers find this to be the most enjoyable portion of the entire process. It is at this point that teacher/researchers systematically look at all the data that have been collected to see what trends or patterns emerge and what conclusions, if any, can be drawn. This is usually accomplished by sorting and organizing (what are often) diverse pieces of data into related categories of major themes, issues, and hypotheses. This process inevitably surfaces trends and patterns and allows the researcher to see areas of significance through both the quality and quantity of data in each category.

Reporting of data. The fourth step—which involves researchers inviting others to peek over their shoulders and learn from their practice—is one of the most powerful and rewarding aspects of the collaborative action research process. For this reason it is imperative that teams of action researchers find as many appropriate forums as possible to share what they are learning about teaching and learning. Many schools have used monthly rotating faculty meetings (each meeting in a different classroom) at which classroom data are disseminated to colleagues. Local school publications (newsletters/journals) and educational fairs also have been utilized as mechanisms to institutionalize the spreading of action research findings.

Action planning. Because the purpose of collaborative action research is to improve professional practice, the process is not complete until plans are put in place that take advantage of what has been learned through the systematic inquiry. Using the findings of collaborative action research to plan and implement school and classroom improvement is the heart of the TQE process. In this way collaborative action research becomes part of a continuous strategic planning effort. By institutionalizing the collaborative action research process, the instructional leader helps make teaching in the school less isolated, more tightly connected to the knowledge bases, and more integrated with quality control.

Managing Time as a Resource

One seemingly universal truth in school administration is that there is never enough time to accomplish all for which a principal is responsible. Certain obligations are inevitably left undone. If one attends to every bureaucratic detail demanded by the central office, the state department of education, and the PTA, the principal would have very little time left to devote to instructional supervision. Likewise, if a principal takes to heart the literature on clinical supervision and endeavors to provide teachers in their school with the copious feedback on classroom instruction they were told to provide by their supervision professors, there won't be much time available left for building the culture and organizational climate that is required for a learning organization to prosper.

This simple truth that there will never be enough time must be accompanied by a leader's acceptance of the corollary truth that everything won't get done. Ultimately, the most important aspect of all this is acknowledging that the decision on what gets done or is left undone is up to the principal. In short, time is a "zero sum" resource. If it is spent one way it is not available to be spent another way. Put in other terms, there is enough time to do anything, but not everything!

The goal for instructional leaders is to spend the finite resource of administrator time where they can get the "greatest bang for the buck." Recall the quality pie charts that were discussed in chapter 2. These can provide a practical guide for determining appropriate time allocations for the instructional leader.

A Quality Pie for Principal Time Allocation

Focusing on three questions will be helpful for the principal who desires to use the development of a quality pie chart to guide the investment of his or her time.

Question #1. "What are the output goals of this organization?" The answer to this question ought to be a direct outgrowth of the analysis of the school profile and strategic plan (chapter 1). For example, the profile could state:

- All students who have attended this school for 3 consecutive years will be performing at or above grade level in reading, math computation, and written expression.
- Serious disciplinary infractions (those necessitating referral to the office) will be reduced by one third per year.

- All students will develop the skills of interdependent cooperative work.

Once a clear and concise list of answers to question #1 has been developed, then the leader must turn attention to question #2.

Question #2. "What processes (throughputs) will be likely to have the most powerful impact on the achievement of these outcomes?" (This corresponds to the proposal column on the STP chart.) For example, there may be logic or evidence to support a belief in the value of:

- Aligning the curriculum with the assessment tools used to determine grade level performance in reading, math computation, and written expression
- Successfully utilizing those instructional strategies that have been shown to produce results in reading, writing, and math (Reading Recovery, Joplin Plan grouping, writing process, use of math manipulatives, etc.)
- Using Glasser's problem-solving approach for the behavioral problems encountered in classrooms, hallways, playgrounds, and the cafeteria
- Utilizing a variety of cooperative learning strategies chosen in accordance with their fit for the students, teacher's style, and content

Once a list of priority production (throughput) processes has been developed, the leader who wishes to be maximally effective will need to shift attention to aligning the resource of leadership time to the critical throughputs identified above. This leads to question #3.

Question #3. "How should leadership's time and attention be distributed among these processes?" Answering this last question is a three-step process:

1. Inventory the leadership behavior that contributes to and/or supports each of the critical throughputs.

Making Quality Decisions Based on Data ✧ 117

2. Audit calendars to draw a picture of the current state of time utilization.
3. Construct an STP chart that suggests processes that will help allocate leadership time to organizational priorities.

Step 1. There is no one best way to succeed with the first step of this process. Keeping current on professional literature is a good place to start. Visiting with colleagues who are serving in schools that are doing an exemplary job in achieving the goals the schools value is another approach (e.g., the Peer-Assisted Leadership program referred to in Chapter 3). Another way that should not be overlooked is asking the teachers in what ways they believe the leader could most profitably contribute to enhancing system effectiveness in implementing the process improvements outlined in the building plan.

Step 2. The resource of time is so fleeting that it is like the change in one's pocket. It has a habit of disappearing quickly without a clue as to where it went. In fact, when people think they remember how they spent their discretionary money, they can be terribly wrong! For this reason it is important for the school leader who wishes to spend time in line with priorities to inventory the use of time in one of two fashions. The best is the use of a time log. A simpler, but less precise, strategy is to conduct the same analysis retrospectively through an examination of one's work calendar. To generate a helpful time log:

- Create a chart like the one in Figure 5.6 dividing the teacher workday (defined as the time when most of the faculty report to school and when most have left for the day) into 15-minute intervals.
- Next note what you were doing at every quarter hour point each day during a 10-school-day period.
- Categorize the entries on your time log under headings that roughly correspond to your major instructional leadership duties. Example: Attending a curriculum committee meeting, conducting an informal classroom observation,

Time	Event	Activity
7:30 a.m.	Teachers arrive	Visiting in faculty room
7:45 a.m.		Call from parent
8:00 a.m.		Checking on substitute
8:15 a.m.		Call from central office
8:30 a.m.		Return parent call
8:45 a.m.		Return police call
9:00 a.m.		In hallways
9:15 a.m.		Call from central office
9:30 a.m.	Activity period	Supervising in gym
9:45 a.m.	Activity period	Supervising in gym
10:00 a.m		Teacher observation (planned)
10:15 a.m.		Teacher observation (planned)
10:30 a.m.		Teacher observation (planned)
10:45 a.m.		Call from parent
11:00 a.m.		Return call from parent
11:15 a.m.	First lunch	Talking with V.P.
11:30 a.m.	First lunch	In cafeteria
11:45 a.m.	Second lunch	In cafeteria
12:00 p.m.	Second lunch	Visiting in faculty room

Figure 5.6. Time Use Log

supervising students, responding to a parent complaint, discussion with an instructional staff member over an instructional matter, discussion with an instructional staff member

Making Quality Decisions Based on Data ✧ 119

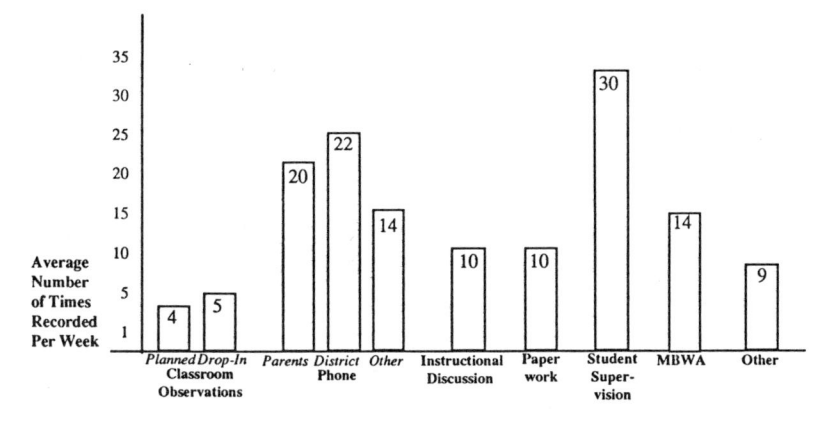

Figure 5.7. Pareto Chart: Principal Time Use

over a noninstructional matter, discussion with a support staff member on an instructional matter, discussion with a support staff member on a noninstructional matter.

- Now construct a *pareto chart* (see Figure 5.7) that displays the use of your time over this 2-week period.
- Then, construct a quality pie that reflects how you feel your time should have been spent if you were applying your most critical leadership resource (your time) to the crucial throughputs for the organization. Note: A school administrator must devote a certain percentage of time to management issues (it is not unreasonable to allocate up to 25% of your time to desk work and other "administrivia"). In addition, a good administrator should allocate time for emergent issues that will inevitably arise, but cannot be accurately anticipated (we would suggest appropriating at least 20% to this purpose). This should leave a minimum of 50% of your time to be divided among what you know to be critical instructional leadership activities.

Step 3. The final step in the process is using the STP chart to construct a personal plan for improvement. To the degree that your time is not being invested in the behaviors that are likely to improve quality, actualize desired outcomes, and minimize variability around optimal levels of performance, the proposal column in the STP chart can be a guide for correction.

It has been said that "an organization is the extended shadow of its leader." Whether or not this is true, it has face validity and its power has been established through collective perception. By this we mean that what people see a leader attending to is what they infer the leader values. What the leader values is (to be hoped) consistent with what the organization values and has articulated in its mission statement (see chapter 1). It is for this reason that what the principal is seen doing will telegraph to the faculty what the school values. Therefore, the TQE principal is wise to orchestrate his or her workday (herein defined as the time when other professionals are in the building) in approximate correspondence to the pie chart described earlier. In the next chapter we will look at ways to get the most out of the time invested with the professional staff.

Key Terms and Concepts

Collaborative action research. A process whereby teams of colleagues conduct investigations into issues of their own practice. Rather than taking a removed posture and examining the work of others, action researchers focus their attention to systematically reflecting on their own work with the goal being to revise practice so that variation can be further reduced.

Creative tension. One's awareness of the gap between the current level of performance and the vision that he or she holds. If one is oriented to produce work of the highest quality, acknowledging that gap will create psychological tension that can be relieved only by the application of creative problem solving.

Pareto chart. A bar graph created to display the relative frequency of occurrences in a person's work or a system. Pareto charts are used to produce statistical quality control.

Reducing variation. A concept that goes to the heart of TQM. The goal of the quality-oriented organization is to reduce the percentage of deviation around the optimal output level. TQM leaders work at reducing variation through the use of statistical quality control mechanisms. For example, if a TQE school determined that students should be able to speak articulately, it would have the goal to reduce to zero the percentage of inarticulate students.

School profile. A purposeful document generated by a school to help clearly understand the current condition in light of organizational goals. A well-constructed profile will serve to generate the creative tension necessary to produce changes in practice.

STP chart. A procedure that can assist a work group in analyzing their current situation (drawn from the profile), contrasting it with their vision, and proposing interventions with a likelihood of closing the gap between current reality and vision.

Time as a resource. The recognition by leadership that one discretionary resource at their command is *where* and *how* they apply the time they spend at work. Effective leaders have learned that the strategic use of available time is a powerful tool at their command.

References

Barth, R. S. (1987). The principal and the profession of teaching. In W. Greenfield (Ed.), *Instructional leadership, concepts, issues, and controversies* (pp. 249-270). Boston: Allyn & Bacon.

Little, J. W. (1982). Norms of collegiality and experimentation: Workplace conditions of school success. *American Educational Research Journal, 19,* 325-340.

NWREL. (1989). *Profiling workbook.* Portland, OR: Northwest Regional Educational Laboratory.

Sagor, R. (1991). Effective schooling: Lessons from the athletic field. *NASSP Bulletin, 75*(534), 95-101.

Sagor, R. (1993). *How to conduct collaborative action research.* Alexandria, VA: ASCD.

Saphier, J., & King, M. (1985). Good seeds grow in strong cultures. *Educational Leadership, 42,* 67-73.

Senge, P. M. (1990). *The fifth discipline: The art and practice of the learning organization.* New York: Doubleday Currency.

✧ 6 ✧

Building a Professional Learning Community

Deming felt that one of the key attributes of a leader was the ability to create trust. As we have discussed throughout this book, adopting the TQM perspective asks the leader to foster a "fear-less" environment. Such environments can only be forged where there is trust in the leader by the workers and where employees are prone to see one another as colleagues rather than as conspirators. This leads to the question of what a principal needs to do to inspire trust with and between the professional educators in the building.

The establishment of trust begins by the leader living up to what has now become a management cliché, "walking the talk." In schools that are committed to achieving total quality, the focus of leadership must be, by definition, teaching and learning. Such schools make a point of "sticking to the knitting" (Peters & Waterman, 1982). If a leader is to be perceived as caring about teaching and learning, then he or she has to be perceived as focusing the resources at command on this aspect of the organization. If a priority pie reveals that the classroom is the most important venue for improvement, then that is where the principal needs to be seen exercising leadership. Effective principals engage in techniques such as making daily drop-in visits to classrooms, doing their paperwork outside of the school day, and regularly attending departmental or grade level meetings.

There are a variety of techniques that have proved helpful for principals who are interested in doing this. All of these strategies are illustrations of the direct supportive behaviors described in chapter 4, particularly conducting frequent classroom visits, constantly communicating with the staff about teaching and learning, and being a visible presence throughout the school building.

To ensure that these types of supportive behaviors occur, instructional leaders must gain control of their calendars. Dedicated administrators find that open space on a calendar has a habit of filling up. For this reason the principal who wants to be ready and available for emergent needs (if and when they arise) must prepare for that availability. Techniques to do this include:

Schedule 1 hour per day for the walk-around. This is best achieved by rotating the allocated time across the full length of the school day. By doing it this way, the walk-around does not seem to be patterned and there will be greater likelihood of finding a variety of things to observe.

It is important that administrators avoid looking at walk-arounds as free time. When the district office calls and asks about a principal's availability for a meeting and the time conflicts with a scheduled walk-around, the principal should be prepared to respond by saying, "I have a conflict at that time." One should be willing to override a prior commitment to a walk-around only if and when it can be rescheduled on the same day or if one confronts a true emergency.

Encourage the scheduling of work-group meetings in a manner that minimizes conflicts. By doing so, the principal (as a limited partner) can usually be available for attending everyone's meeting. A school's work group meeting schedule might look something like this:

1st grade: Monday before school
2nd grade: Monday after school
3rd grade: Tuesday before school
4th grade: Tuesday after school
5th grade: Wednesday before school
6th grade: Wednesday after school
Faculty meetings: Thursday before school

Kindergarten: Thursday after school
Specialists: Friday before school

Although groups should not be required to meet every week (unless there is business to transact) and it should not be mandated that folks meet only at the appointed time, attention to this type of schedule will make it more likely that the principal (or for that matter any interested party) could attend any meeting about which they have an interest.

Practice looking "less than overwhelmed." These days the typical posture struck by school administrators looks remarkably similar to that attributed to the Greek god Atlas, crippled as a result of carrying the weight of the world on his shoulders. Although striking this pose may engender sympathy and admiration, it also becomes a block to open communication. Employees and other compassionate people are reluctant to bring up their needs and to interrupt someone if that person already appears overwhelmed. By looking ready and available, leaders telegraph the message that their job is no more important than the responsibilities of the teachers with whom they work.

Management by Walking Around

Although this technique is widely recognized and promoted as an effective management strategy, it involves far more than just wandering around aimlessly. This powerful technique is explored at length in *School Management by Wandering Around* by L. Frase and R. Hetzel. To make the most of management by walking around (MBWA) a principal needs to be cognizant of three things: what to look for, what to comment on, and what to do when one is out and about.

MBWA is a self-reinforcing technique. If one does it infrequently, it not only fails to achieve desired ends, but can even be an unpleasant activity. When a principal who is rarely seen out of the office walks into a classroom, folks are prone to stop what they are doing and ask, "What do you want?" or "Can I help you?" This can make a principal feel awkward, especially if the only answer that comes to mind is, "Nothing, I'm just wandering around." Conversely, once people have become accustomed to seeing their principal around and about and dropping in here and there, then the principal's presence becomes seen as normative and no one will be inclined to stop what he or she is doing on account of the leader's arrival. So what should a principal do when out and about?

Whether at the elementary, middle, or high school levels, the most respected adult behavior in schools is (and should be) the act of teaching. More important, when principals engage in teaching and are seen as enjoying instruction as well as being comfortable with it, they bond themselves to the teaching corps. It is for this reason that the "wandering principal" is well served to seek out opportunities to roll up his or her sleeves and help students with school work wherever and whenever possible.

A study of effective principals (Sagor, 1992) observed individuals who were in every classroom in their schools at least once and often several times a day. When these leaders crossed the classroom threshold no one reacted because it was such a normal occurrence. Because of their familiarity with both the students and the academic programs operating in their buildings, these principals were able to jump right in and help students with any difficulties they were experiencing. By doing this on a regular basis these principals became partners with each of their teachers on two critical aspects of the teacher's work: the education of individual students and the management of the school's instructional program.

Even though we have suggested that principals try to master looking less than overwhelmed, it is still a good idea for leaders to carry a notepad when wandering. The pad serves two important purposes. Wandering is much like the morning shower, in that it becomes a time when one is open to all sorts of fortuitous insights. The notepad gives the leader a chance to capture these insights before they are forgotten (this usually doesn't work well in the shower because ink has a tendency to run).

Another good reason to carry a notepad is the opportunity it provides for writing notes to staff members as appropriate. Consider these factors:

1. The main work of the organization is teaching and learning.
2. If a school is committed to continuous progress, then it is in the classrooms where that commitment is most often demonstrated.
3. If one critical role for management in a TQM environment is keeping people focused on their collective vision, then capturing people doing inspiring and successful things in the classroom and drawing staff attention to the principal's knowledge about and interest in the work of teachers is one of the most important things a TQE instructional leader can do.

Frequently when walking around for an hour a principal will encounter up to a half dozen examples of excellent work. Those examples can be acknowledged with short and simple handwritten notes. For example:

John,
I was shocked to see how well Emma was paying attention in math today. I would be interested in finding out what strategy you used to get her involved. No one else seems to be having similar success with her.
Keep up the good work!

Ellisa,
I was truly impressed with the way you managed the debate on reproductive choice in your class today. Sometime you need to share your technique for dealing with controversial issues with the rest of the faculty. It was truly masterful!

The principal who wanders frequently will be peppering many a faculty mailbox with those type of notes. The reasons why this is successful are:

1. Handwritten notes imply a sincerity that is missed in both oral and typewritten communication.
2. Compliments that are specific seem neither ingratiating nor perfunctory.

3. Notes reinforce the shared organizational commitment to instructional quality.

Governance

In the current era of school reform, too many governance initiatives seem to be started with a "one size fits all" philosophy. Principals committed to a TQE approach would be wise to avoid falling into this trap. Many site-based management initiatives were born out of the acknowledgment that teachers did not want to be subjected to uninspiring and ineffective administration. As a defense against this teachers agreed (even demanded) a meaningful say in decision making. Too infrequently the site-based management solution is as bad as the disease it was introduced to cure. The authoritative role of the principal can be just as easily replaced by an overly procedural governance process that has the faculty collectively deliberating over matters of both great and minimal import. Not only do such approaches fail to bring greater quality outcomes, but they can also have a deleterious impact on morale. After all, teachers usually want to teach; if they wanted to be managers they would be getting a license that enables them to do so.

The key for the TQE school leader is to involve people in the matters that they care to be consulted on and to handle the other matters in the most efficient method possible. In practical terms this means to put in place a governance process that can be utilized in a contingent fashion. For example, decision-making processes might be categorized along an involvement continuum:

Executive decision
Committee decision (volunteers)
Representative decision
Plebiscite
Consensus

Clearly, the most efficient and fastest approach is the executive decision. It takes very little time and involves a minimum number of people. Generally people enjoy living and working in an organization where wise executive decisions are the rule. Unfortunately, the supply of philosopher-kings isn't what it used to be.

On the other extreme is consensus. Its beauty lies in the fact that everyone agrees with the outcome. But the cost of reaching agreement often is either an enormous investment of time or the compromise of principle and passion. The key for the total quality leader is choosing when to use which decision-making strategy.

Tannenbaum and Schmidt (1957) provided a conceptual mechanism for making that choice by employing the reasoning contained in a schema they called "zones of indifference" (see Figure 6.1).

The leader who understands the organizational culture of his or her school will quickly become adept at determining which decisions fall where on this chart. The strategies outlined in chapter 3 about reading the present culture and shaping a culture more consistent with the school's vision can be particularly useful in determining how the decision-making process is working or ought to work. Nevertheless, even with a leader with good instincts at the helm, a good governance system is one that acknowledges that errors in the selection of a decision-making process can and (probably) will be made. Therefore, it is understood that the faculty can always ask for the referral of any decision that was made too far over on the authoritative end to one of the more inclusive or participatory approaches. For example, assume that the principal believed that a decision on what constituted permissible playground behavior could and should be made by the student management committee (a voluntary ad hoc faculty group). When the decision of the group was reported at a faculty meeting, significant dissent was expressed (to the principal's surprise). Many teachers shared their desire for more involvement in the process. An appropriate principal reaction would be to say, "I see that we misjudged faculty concern on this topic. Therefore, we will suspend this decision and refer the matter for consideration of the total faculty at our next meeting." Once such an approach is institutionalized it tells the community that everyone's opinion and time is respected and valued.

INCREASES ◄——— ZONE OF INDIFFERENCE ———► DECREASES

Use of Authority
By the Principal

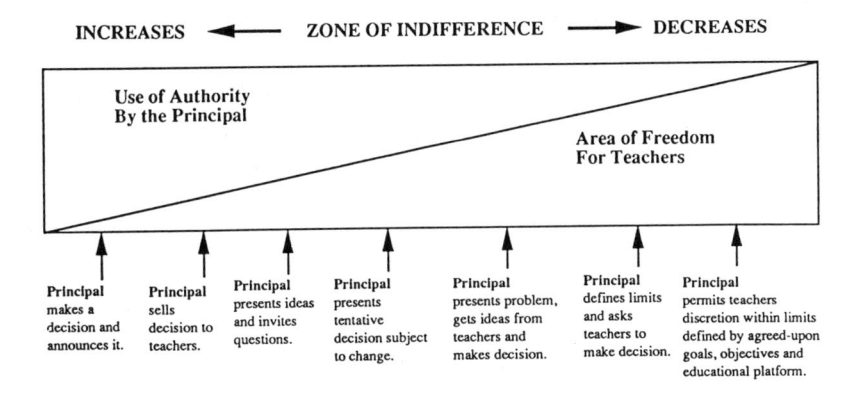

Area of Freedom
For Teachers

| Principal makes a decision and announces it. | Principal sells decision to teachers. | Principal presents ideas and invites questions. | Principal presents tentative decision subject to change. | Principal presents problem, gets ideas from teachers and makes decision. | Principal defines limits and asks teachers to make decision. | Principal permits teachers discretion within limits defined by agreed-upon goals, objectives and educational platform. |

Figure 6.1. Decision-Making Continuum

SOURCE: Adapted from "How to Choose a Leadership Pattern" by Robert Tannenbaum and Warren Schmidt, 1957, *Harvard Business Review, 36*(2).

Not Expecting Perfection

Deming warns employers to avoid expecting perfection. It is not that he doubts the value of high expectations, but he is cognizant of the negative consequences that flow from expecting or being seen as demanding superhuman efforts from mere mortals. There are several reasons for this. If, as Deming asserts, 85% of a system's performance is due to factors outside of personnel, then demanding perfection from employees is patently unreasonable. But more important, an expectation of flawless performance gives workers an incentive to lie and mislead both their colleagues and supervisors on the quality of their work. Fear inevitably breeds distrust, and distrust then breeds dishonesty.

One way out of the perfection expectation problem is to shift the quality control burden downward in the organization. External quality control officers have been shown to be problematic in a number of ways:

1. They take the focus away from systemic concerns (see chapter 2). By focusing on the outputs rather than the through-

puts the data produced by traditional supervisors are of little diagnostic value.
2. They enhance the alienation of the worker from the product of his or her labor. After all, if work of poor quality is accepted because the quality control officer fell asleep on the job or has low standards, then how important was producing quality anyhow?
3. Over time the reliance on the external quality control officer breeds an external locus of control on the part of the worker.

There is, however, a powerful mechanism at the principal's control that can help avoid the reliance on the external quality control officer. It extends the benefits of collaborative action research that were explored in chapter 5. It is the conscious and strategic use of *cognitive dissonance* (Festinger, 1964). Before covering the strategic use of this phenomenon, we will conduct a quick review of this law of behavioral psychology.

Cognitive Dissonance Theory

Point 1: Human beings constantly engage in behavior. As people act, live, breathe, and behave they hold attitudes about behavior. They either like or dislike the car they drive, they enjoy or are depressed by their work, they believe the clothes they are wearing are either flattering or make them look bad.

Point 2: Humans have a natural aversion to stress. One source of stress for people is the realization that their behavior and attitudes are in conflict. For example: The smoker who believes the surgeon general is correct on the health hazards of tobacco will be under stress. The soldier who believes in nonviolence will be in an uncomfortable position when sent into combat.

Cognitive dissonance theory argues that when attitudes and behavior are in conflict people tend to experience heightened anxiety and stress. For example, if a chain-smoker has internalized the totality of the surgeon general's warning on cigarette smoking, then the act of lighting up and inhaling each cigarette places that smoker in an increased state of stress, because with each breath the smoker consciously reminds himself or herself that this behavior is likely leading to life-threatening consequences. This phenomenon can be expressed by the following equation:

Attitude and Behavior in Conflict (Dissonant) = Stress

However, when attitudes and behaviors are in agreement (consonant), stress is reduced. It is for this reason that chain-smokers frequently hold the attitude, "What the surgeon general says may be true for most people, but it simply doesn't apply to me." This state of cognitive consonance is expressed with another equation:

Attitude and Behavior Congruent = Reduced Stress

Figure 6.2 illustrates the way this phenomenon gets played out in a typical school.

Psychologists have traditionally referred to dissonance as the relationship between two factors—attitude and behavior. However, when this phenomenon is applied to the social reality of the schoolhouse, it is important to add the dimension of role. This is because, due to adults' affiliation needs, faculty peer culture is another powerful force influencing teacher change.

Why is understanding and managing dissonance important for effective TQE principals? The answer comes from an examination of the change process as explicated by the preeminent American psychologist Kurt Lewin. Although change is a personal experience (see chapter 2), Lewin (1948) offered a well-reasoned conception of why organizations (like schools) seem so resistant to change. He explained it through the concept of the *force field*. Basically, a force field illustrates the balancing of opposing forces regarding any specific change in practice.

A force field explains why the modus operandi operates as it does in many organizations or why any particular traditional practice sustains itself. For example, the way all the everyday

132 ✧ The TQE Principal: A Transformed Leader

Figure 6.2. Cognitive Dissonance Cycle

things are done in your school—how attendance is handled, how the playground is supervised, how rank in class is derived, how the daily schedule works—were arrived at because there once was a standoff. The point of the standoff was that place where the forces pushing for more progressive change were approximately offset by the forces desiring the implementation of a more regressive approach. The point where the pressure for change and the pressure to resist the same change were approximately equal was the point where the status quo was established. This is a state Lewin called "frozen."

The only way to get past the standoff represented by the balancing of forces for and forces against is to find a way to unbalance the equation. Effective leaders do this by presenting data or questions that will fundamentally challenge preexisting assumptions, beliefs, or attitudes.

For example, suppose a secondary school had institutionalized a philosophy that held that only a select few students could

Forces For
Some students succeed with calculus
Some students respond to challenges
Some students apply themselves in class
Some students do homework diligently

Forces Against
Some students fail basic math
Some students quit when it gets rough
Some students abuse class time
Many students don't complete homework

Figure 6.3. Force Field on Mathematics

effectively handle the study of the advanced math curriculum of calculus. A chart like the one in Figure 6.3 might illustrate the beliefs that led to that conclusion.

Now suppose the faculty at this school just learned of the results obtained at Garfield High School in East Los Angeles by Jaime Escalante and his colleagues. The natural response would be to look for explanations of these new data in light of their previously held beliefs. Or in the terms that futurist Joel Barker (1992) popularized, look for answers that line up with the prevailing paradigm. A math department might suspect that the performance obtained at Garfield was the result of factors such as the students coming to high school with superior math backgrounds, using better text materials, taking easier tests, or cheating to improve their results.

But as the data on Escalante's students are scrutinized it will become clear to this faculty that none of those easy explanations will hold up. The Garfield students entered high school weak in math skills, they utilized texts that were in widespread use elsewhere, they took the same test that was administered nationally, and investigators concluded that their tests were taken individually and honestly. Once rejecting those arguments the suspicious math teachers will be left with only one possible explanation for these data: Apparently the math instruction (e.g., teaching techniques) utilized at Garfield was better than that utilized at their

134 ✧ **The TQE Principal: A Transformed Leader**

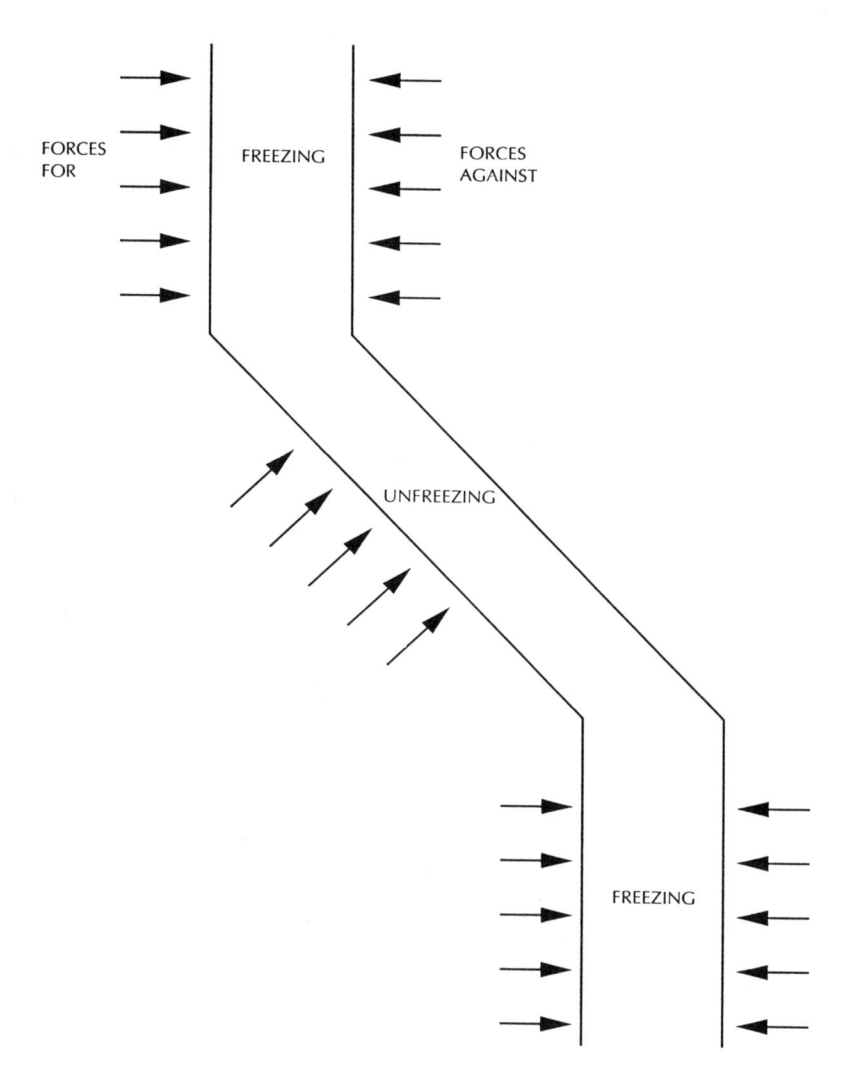

Figure 6.4. Effect of Compelling Data on the Force Field

school. Such realizations cause the melting away of one half of the equation (Figure 6.4), thereby allowing the forces for change to shift unimpeded.

The effective instructional leader is an individual who has learned to use this phenomenon to the school's advantage. But doing so will require mastery of certain skills or what Peter Senge calls "disciplines."

Having a Clear Vision of the Quality School

The effective instructional leader and those who are in the leader's employ must operate with a clear view of the quality school that they hope to build. Although that vision may be constantly subject to revision, the current understanding of that vision should be a picture perceived with great clarity. Methods for establishing this vision were explored more fully in chapter 1. However, once a vision is established it should live just beyond the horizon of current reality. Between the vision and current reality is a gulf. This gulf may be thought of metaphorically as containing the chasm that lies between the opposing positions of the force field. Getting people to want to cross that gulf is the essence of creating and managing creative tension (see chapter 5).

The thinking of the leader strategizing to bridge this gulf is analogous to the planning conducted by a military commander or football coach. When Eisenhower contemplated the invasion of Normandy (a task he wanted to accomplish with minimal Allied casualties) his goal was to go where the enemy wasn't. This is the essential purpose of military reconnaissance: to scan the environment to find the path of least resistance. That will not always necessarily be the shortest distance between two points or the route one would take if serious obstacles were not anticipated. Rather, it is the route that one chooses to travel because taking it will produce the least negative consequences.

A football coach constructing a game plan finds himself in pretty much the same boat. The coach's vision is clear: a scoreboard at the end of the game showing more points for the home team than for the opponent. To accomplish that goal will require more than simply inventorying the strengths of his team (the forces for) but also a consideration of the defense that will be encountered (the forces against). If a scouting report (the athletic version of reconnaissance) reflects a weakness in the opposing team's defense, the smart coach will design a game plan that exploits that weakness.

Effective instructional leaders are engaged in similar work; they must know the internal and external (forces against) sitting between the vision and current reality and effectively plan to move where ground is given or "where the enemy ain't." To do this requires two things: knowing where you are going (vision) and knowing the terrain.

Simply put, the management of dissonance is a method for leaders to test and/or soften forces against change. Although this process is relatively easy to describe, it requires an enormous amount of administrative finesse. When becoming a manager of dissonance there are certain things a leader should try to remember and other things a leader will be wise to avoid. Things to remember:

1. Keep a clear picture of your target in your mind's eye at all times. This requires understanding your vision with all its nuances. By seeing your picture with clarity opportunities can be spotted and cul-de-sacs can be avoided.
2. The people you work with have an investment in their conception of current reality. Don't expect rational people to abandon their beliefs absent a confrontation with compelling data that bring those beliefs into question.

Things to avoid:

1. Don't be unfocused.
2. Don't debate beliefs.
3. Don't ridicule resisters.
4. Don't invite opposition.

A Case in Point

Consider the case of a high school principal in which the faculty was crafting a vision of a school with high rates of student success. Without investing much time in group process the principal began to focus on the grades awarded to students as the critical piece of outcome data. A few months after the "success initiative" began, semester grades were awarded. The principal analyzed student grades by teacher and presented them in a report to the faculty at an in-service meeting. Among the handouts was a faculty roster with the percentage of failure grades awarded. Next to the name of each teacher was either a smiley face (indicating a low percentage of F's) or a "frowny" face (indicative of a high percentage of failures). Many influential members of the faculty were deeply offended by this heavy-handed treatment and as a consequence hardened their opposition to the success initiative.

This case study indicates the importance of the factors listed above. The vision of a school with successful students had not been clearly understood or visualized by either the principal or his faculty. Prematurely assuming that grades ought to be the critical indicator of the type of school they were creating was one of their problems. The data used (percentage of failure grades) were not compelling enough to defrost the forces against. In fact, it was so off-target as to be dismissed by faculty with comments like: "It is easy to improve our grades, if that's what they want; we'll just lower our standards," and "If it's high grades he wants, we'll give them to him."

Finally, this principal behaved in a manner that was easily interpreted as ridiculing important members of the school community. This was a significant mistake that served to harden previous positions. More important, the decisions made by this principal demonstrated weak skills in environmental scanning. The teachers' defensiveness about grades was functionally equivalent to antiaircraft batteries set up to defend a beach or defensive backs prepared to cover wide receivers. Rather than going where the defense was weak, this principal drove headfirst right into the opposition. As a consequence his forces sustained dramatically increased casualties.

An Alternative Example

Clyde was a principal at a middle school where the faculty had a clear vision of a "high-success, child-centered, caring environment." This faculty described itself as a community that "wouldn't allow a student to fail." Historically, this school had tracked students into ability groups, a practice that ran counter to Clyde's vision and that of many of the newly hired staff. Tracking, however, did not violate the collective vision of a high-success, child-centered, caring school as understood by many of the pro–ability-grouping faculty. Rather these people saw tracking as affording them the opportunity to meet individual needs, to provide remediation and support, and to make the curriculum better fit the learners.

The principal helped the faculty see that tracking was not (in itself) a critical piece of their mission. Rather, he argued that it should be seen as either a good or bad means (throughput) to achieve their shared vision. In other words, grouping decisions were means, not ends. As a result, the faculty reasoned if they truly cared to produce their collective shared vision, it would be helpful to examine alternative routes. As a result this faculty engaged in collaborative action research (see chapter 5) to surface data on the efficacy of ability grouping for their school. Several pilot-detracked classes were begun while many of the ability-grouped classes continued. Data on self-esteem, perseverance, and learning were collected. Once the data were assembled and analyzed the faculty discussed what the data implied about the efficacy of these two alternative approaches to instructional organization.

The data were inconclusive. Most all the students did well (as one might have expected when being taught by such a caring faculty). However, the faculty decided to detrack. This consensus decision was reached with mutual respect and without acrimony because (a) the collective vision was clear and shared; (b) positions, beliefs, and values were respected—not ridiculed—and compelling data were obtained; and (c) the data, not the principal, ultimately served to weaken existing defenses against change.

How to Create a Learning Community

Taking all of the ideas presented in this book about Total Quality Education and the transformed instructional leader, we can see that the hallmark of the TQE school is that it is a learning community. This is important on two counts. First, the principles of total quality management emphasize continuous improvement. Continuous improvement implies a constant inquiry into what is being worked on (the inputs), how it is being done (the throughputs), and what results are obtained (the outputs).

Followers of Deming will recognize the continuous improvement process in his famous circular Plan-Do-Study-Act (PDSA) cycle. The PDSA cycle illustrates the way an organization makes continuous improvement a never-ending fact of life. In schools this is accomplished by institutionalizing the five-step action research process outlined in chapter 5 (problem formulation, data collection, analysis, reporting, modifying practice). Although it seems like a small thing, the factor that differentiates this approach from traditional efforts at school improvement is the recognition that the process is circular, not linear. The importance of this distinction cannot be overemphasized.

In schools teachers may think of their roles as investigating a technique until they learn to do it right. That perspective runs counter to the essence of the learning community. The school that believes it already has all the answers is unlikely to become or stay an excellent enterprise. Conversely, the school that continues to examine these issues will continue to prosper. Carl Glickman has asserted that the improving schools are the ones that claim, "We don't ever expect to get it right, but we do expect to keep doing it better" (Glickman, 1993a, 1993b).

The Willamette Elementary School in West Linn, Oregon, has taken this notion to heart and has created an informal school symbol, the international stop sign with an *it* in the center. With this symbol this faculty is giving testimony to their internalization of Michael Fullan's (Fullan & Stiegelbauer, 1991) assertion that change is "a journey, not a destination."

The most important reason for a TQE school to commit itself to becoming a learning community is the dynamic relationship of process to product. Students learn more from how adults behave than by what they say. Students will learn to be thinkers and inquirers only if they see adults behaving as thinkers and inquirers.

The question then becomes how does or can a principal lead a school toward becoming a genuine learning community? The answer is by casting him- or herself as the lead student. This can be done in a variety of ways that have been described in this book, specifically:

- Conducting and sharing action research
- Participating in limited partnerships
- Showing interest in others' learning
- Creating opportunities for collaborative adult learning
- Modeling lifelong learning

Creating such a learning community does not happen overnight. The transformed instructional leader must not only understand the whole using systemic thinking, but also realize how the different parts of the system contribute to or detract from the school's vision. This is quite a different approach than merely tinkering with individual, isolated components of the school organization. Therefore, patience is perhaps the greatest virtue these instructional leaders must possess. By using a systems approach, understanding the change process, and attempting to read and shape the culture to create a community of learners, instructional leaders need to know their efforts will not always proceed as quickly as they would like. They must constantly celebrate successes, no matter how minor, and keep vigil over the vision or direction of the school.

Key Terms and Concepts

Cognitive dissonance. The psychological theory that explains how human beings reconcile conflicts between attitudes and behavior. To reduce stress people have a tendency to try to bring attitudes and behavior in line with each other by changing whichever is easier to adjust.

Decision-making continuum. A leader can choose to have governance decisions made by an array of strategies, from those that maximize participation and are therefore rather slow, to ones that are quick and decisive but involve the delegation of authority. The effective leader uses a strategic analysis to determine when to use which approach.

Force field. A pictorial way to display the factors that are supporting or resisting any change effort. Analysis of a force field can help leaders understand what factors need to be altered or addressed to make the occurrence of positive change more likely.

Management by walking around (MBWA). A technique whereby leadership asserts itself by being visible in the workplace. When managing by walking around the leader needs to be deliberate about what to look for, what to comment on, and what behaviors to engage in.

Management of dissonance. One of the fine arts of leadership in which the leader deliberately creates a behavior/attitude conflict to elicit creative tension. When done well the discomfiture of the dissonance is the stimulus for improvements in practice.

Plan-Do-Study-Act (PDSA) cycle. This model developed by Deming illustrates the continuous cycle of improvement that comes from an immersion in the data-based decision-making process. It is the method whereby the TQM organization makes use of action research.

Shifting the quality control burden. Traditional managers played the external quality control function. This breeds distrust within organizations. The modern TQM manager is one who has learned to avoid expecting perfection, but rather expects continuous improvement. This is handled by delegating the quality control function to the level of the organization conducting the work.

References

Barker, J. A. (1992). *Future edge: Discovering the new paradigms of success.* New York: William Morrow.

Festinger, L. (1964). *Conflict, decision, and dissonance.* Stanford, CA: Stanford University Press.

Frase, L. , & Hetzel, R. (1990). *School Management by Wandering Around.* Lancaster, PA: Technomic.

Fullan, M., & Stiegelbauer, S. (1991). *The new meaning of educational change.* New York: Teachers College Press.

Glickman, C. D. (1993a, March). *Promoting good schools: The core of professional work.* Paper presented at the conference of the Association for Supervision and Curriculum Development, Washington, DC.

Glickman, C. D. (1993b). *Renewing America's schools: A guide for school based action.* San Francisco: Jossey-Bass.

Lewin, K. (1948). *Resolving social conflicts.* New York: Harper & Brothers.

Peters, T. J., & Waterman, R. H., Jr. (1982). *In search of excellence: Lessons from America's best-run companies.* New York: Harper & Row.

Sagor, R. (1992). Operationalizing transformational leadership: Three principals who make a difference. *Educational Leadership, 49,* 13-18.

Tannenbaum, R., & Schmidt, W. (1957). How to choose a leadership pattern. *Harvard Business Review, 36*(2), 96.

❖ 7 ❖

A TQE Model of Instructional Leadership

In this book we have discussed a number of the principles raised by Deming and others as crucial for leadership in a TQM environment. Each of the models of leadership and techniques that we have presented could be utilized in isolation by principals who wish to develop the people and/or programs in their school. However, the power in these ideas becomes amplified when they are integrated into a comprehensive plan for total quality school leadership. In this concluding chapter we attempt to put each of the critical elements presented in this book into a unified model of instructional leadership for Total Quality Education.

In the Beginning . . .

Scripture says where there is no vision the people perish. This also is true in schools. The road to total quality must begin with a shared agreement on the destination. This is why we started this book with an examination of the strategic planning process. Strategic planning is not an imprecise or ephemeral exercise. Rather, it is a process aimed at defining clear targets that are to be obtained at a specified point in time. Strategic planning had its origins in the manufacturing sector where suppliers needed to have accurate understandings of the particular products that their customers wanted and needed to have available on a certain date. This focus on the customer was deemed essential to any company that wanted to increase or maintain a substantial market share. Most important, these companies found that strategic planning worked! They observed that when their engineering departments knew the targets they were after (even when they didn't yet know the way to get there) they could, in relatively short order, create plans that enabled the target to be achieved. The same holds true for schools. Strategic planning can enable a faculty to agree on where they want to be in the future with enough precision to inform decision making on action plans.

Perilous Roads Shouldn't Be Traveled Alone . . .

The second chapter of this book explored several mechanisms to encourage the productive functioning of professional work groups. It is not that individual educators are incapable of doing good work by themselves, but in total quality schools the whole is inevitably more than the sum of its parts. Traditional manufacturing industries have found that when teams of workers are given the power to make important decisions regarding their work and when they are responsible for quality control, both productivity and worker satisfaction tend to increase. This is even more true in schools, where faculty members are more likely to be affiliation motivated. Hence, the total quality principal intuitively realizes that if he or she wants to have the school move rapidly and deliberately in the direction of continuous progress, it will require more than just a shared mission, vision, set of goals, and clarity on objectives. It also becomes critical to encourage and empower collegial work groups to work creatively and collaboratively to generate solutions to the organization's problems. We have suggested employing strategies such as DIP/GLIP to cause the entire professional staff to engage in limited partnerships with the principal to advance the school's strategic plan.

Slogans Are Not Enough . . .

This is not the first time in education that people have heard calls for more collaboration and collegiality. Likewise, it is not the first time that it has been suggested to educators that they focus their work on the achievement of long-range goals or visions. Nevertheless, despite a long history of these admonitions, most well-intended reform efforts have unraveled. Among the reasons for this is the fact that little attention has been paid to the skills and knowledge necessary to help groups of professionals work successfully. The principal who wants to preside over a total quality school will need to place the support of staff in acquiring the skills of collegiality as one of their top leadership goals. This means several things.

First, leaders need to help develop an organizational ethos that respects continuous improvement and places an emphasis on staff development. Second, the staff development effort must make strategic use of locally derived data on which decisions appropriate for the local context can be crafted. Toward this end principals must learn how to lead the faculty into peer coaching and peer supervision activities. In addition, we suggest that they encourage participation in the process of collaborative action research and that they be able to lead efforts to construct school profiles that can be used as part of an ongoing strategic planning process.

Do as You Say or "Walk Your Talk" . . .

Leadership in the total quality school must recognize that the way the adults in a school conduct their business is as instructive as the lessons they elect to directly teach. For example, if the governance process fails to respect the input of all school citizens and if the attitude of the veteran teachers implies they have largely learned all that there is to know, then the continuous search for better ways to reduce the variation around optimum output will be futile and the ownership of innovations and interventions will be less than desired.

Figure 7.1 illustrates the interactive model of instructional leadership promoted in this book. The model respects the importance of three pillars of a TQE school:

- Being vision driven
- Being data based
- Being people powered

146 ✧ **The TQE Principal: A Transformed Leader**

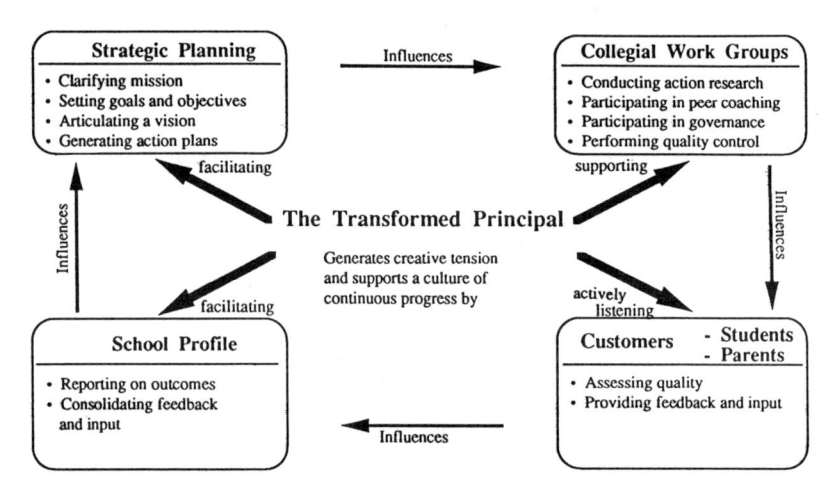

```
┌─────────────────────────────┐                              ┌─────────────────────────────┐
│   Strategic Planning        │      Influences              │   Collegial Work Groups     │
│ • Clarifying mission        │ ───────────────►             │ • Conducting action research│
│ • Setting goals and objectives                             │ • Participating in peer coaching
│ • Articulating a vision     │                              │ • Participating in governance
│ • Generating action plans   │                              │ • Performing quality control│
└─────────────────────────────┘                              └─────────────────────────────┘
              facilitating                                          supporting
                                  The Transformed Principal
                                  Generates creative tension
                                  and supports a culture of
              facilitating        continuous progress by      actively listening
┌─────────────────────────────┐                              ┌─────────────────────────────┐
│   School Profile            │                              │   Customers   - Students    │
│                             │                              │               - Parents     │
│ • Reporting on outcomes     │                              │ • Assessing quality         │
│ • Consolidating feedback    │                              │ • Providing feedback and input
│   and input                 │      Influences              │                             │
└─────────────────────────────┘ ◄───────────────             └─────────────────────────────┘
```

Figure 7.1. A TQE Instructional Leadership Model

No one component of this model can be ignored and, like Deming's PDSA cycle, the improvement process must be continuous. In fact, we believe this model should be seen as seamless. For example, strategic planning is never complete. Plans should constantly be updated as new data from school profiles reflect both new accomplishments and new targets. Each new advance produced as a result of staff development becomes an opportunity to open up new vistas of professional growth opportunities, and each outcome target achieved must be viewed as a plateau offering firm ground from which to mount the next initiative.

If one takes this model to heart there will be two steps ahead for the TQE-oriented school principal. The first is developing and/or strengthening a set of cultural norms—specifically, focusing on the customer, holding high expectations, using data to make decisions, and valuing collaborative work. Once these cultural changes have been accomplished the leader will not feel that the work is done. Rather, once the tradition and expectation of continuous improvement have been institutionalized in a school, then the leader will find his or her role transformed into something even more exhilarating. This is because working in a school culture that values the TQE philosophy invites a faculty and their leaders into an ever-changing, ever-improving, and ever more meaningful terrain. A TQE school is never boring and, as in the corporate world, no one ever gets tired of serving satisfied customers.

Planning and Troubleshooting Guide

Adults as Learners
How do adults react to change?	21-22
How to reduce stress	130-131
Principles of adults' learning	51-54
Reducing dissonance in adults' thinking	130-132
What motivates adults?	22-23

Capitalizing on Teachers' Talents
How to create a collegial learning environment	59-61
How to develop teacher leaders:	
Types of decisions teachers can make	61-62
What concerns do teacher leaders have?	63-67
Involving teachers in collaborative action research:	
Improving quality control in teaching	108-110
Increasing teachers' knowledge	107-108
Reducing teachers' isolation	106-107
What are the steps in collaborative action research?	113-114
What is collaborative action research?	111-112

Continuous Improvement
Creating readiness	30
Departmental and grade level improvement processes	31-34
How can principals model continuous improvement?	30, 140

Planning and Troubleshooting Guide ✧ 149

How can principals provide direct support to teachers?	72-74, 78-81
How to use the Plan-Do-Study-Act cycle	139
Indirect support principals can provide teachers	74-76, 78-81
Institutionalizing continuous improvement	106-114
Peer coaching:	
How is coaching different than evaluation?	82-83, 84
How to train and support coaches	89-93
Observation and feedback strategies coaches can use	83-89
What are the different approaches to coaching?	77, 80-82
Providing successful continuous improvement experiences	29-34

Culture

Creating norms for a learning community	59-61
How can the current culture be "read"?	56-58
How the induction process can socialize new employees to the school's norms	45-47
How to institutionalize continuous improvement in the culture	59-61
Ways to shape the culture	57

Prioritizing and Managing Time and Resources

Management by walking around	124-127
Priority pies:	
How to manage time using a priority pie	115-117
Steps in creating priority pies	24
What do priority pies look like?	26-28
What value is a priority pie?	25

Strategic Planning

Creating action plans	8-9
Creating belief statements	4
Conducting external and internal analyses	5-6
Determining essential policies	7
Determining strategies to accomplish each objective	7-8

Developing measurable objectives 7
Developing mission statements 5
Role of the planning and action teams 3-4, 8-10

Systemic Thinking
How to analyze the system using:
    Educational platforms 14-17
    Force field analysis 131-135
    School profiles 100-104
    Situation-Target-Proposal charts 103-106
How to involve "customers" in assessing
    outcomes 27-28
How to reduce variations in output 97-100
What are inputs, throughputs, and outputs? 24
What is systems thinking? 20-21
Who are the school's customers? 23-24

Vision
How can the hiring process be used to reinforce
    shared values? 43-45
How to buffer external threats to the vision 35-42
How to keep the vision at the forefront 66, 135-136
Ways to create visions:
    Creating educational platforms 14-15
    Developing vision statements 13-14
    Systematic approach to creating a vision 12-17
What is a vision? 10-11
What is the difference between a vision
    and a mission? 5